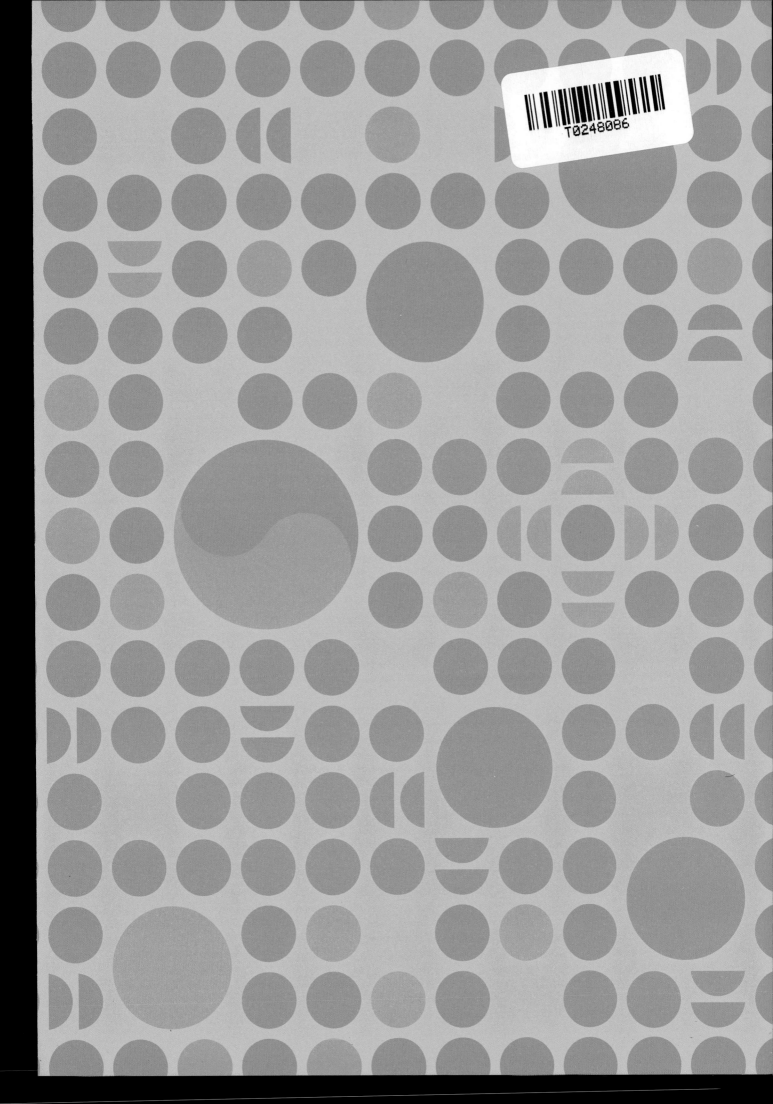

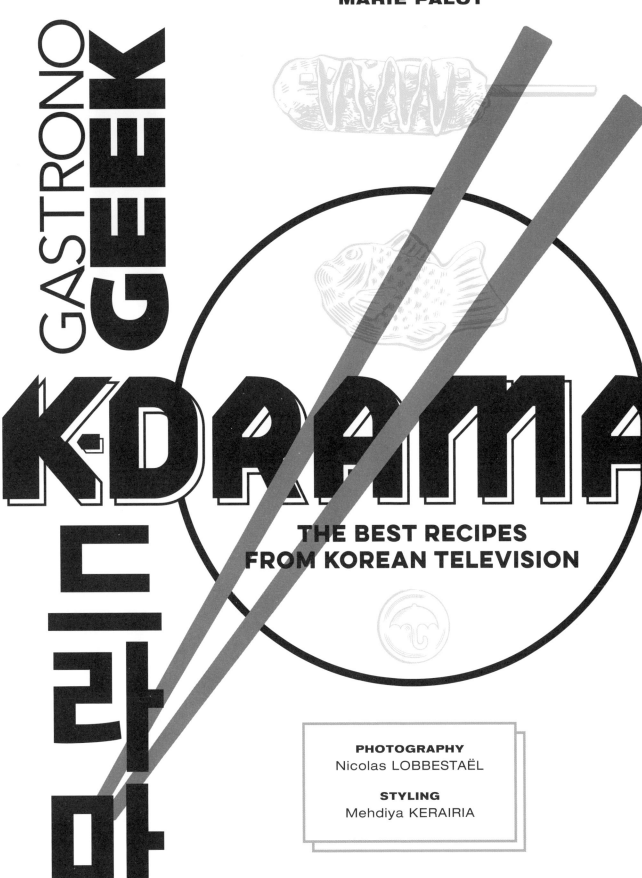

THIBAUD VILLANOVA
MARIE PALOT

GASTRONO
GEEK

K-DRAMA

THE BEST RECIPES
FROM KOREAN TELEVISION

드라마
의 맛

PHOTOGRAPHY
Nicolas LOBBESTAËL

STYLING
Mehdiya KERAIRIA

INSIGHT EDITIONS

SAN RAFAEL · LOS ANGELES · LONDON

MEET THIBAUD VILLANOVA

Welcome to the cookbook that will have you falling in love with the best Korean dramas, whether you're seeing them for the first time or rediscovering them with fresh eyes. Welcome to the latest from Gastronogeek!

With more than fifteen cookbooks under my belt now, it's getting hard to write an introduction without seeming pompous to those who are getting to know me for the first time, or repetitive to those who already own the whole collection.

If we haven't met before, let me just say that ten years ago, I created and started to develop a style of cooking rooted in pop culture, in the broadest sense of the term. My work with Gastronogeek consists of creating and reproducing the dishes you see in your favorite movies, TV shows, and games, as well as the ones you read about or imagine in your favorite manga, novels, and comics. I like to think that by letting you eat the same foods as your heroes and heroines, I also allow you to linger a little longer in these pop culture worlds that you—and I—love so much.

Through this work, since 2014 I've had the honor of publishing more than fifteen cookbooks celebrating cult anime hits, blockbuster genre films, and iconic video games. If you go to a bookstore, you can find my official cookbooks inspired by everything from Disney films, *Astérix*, and Star Wars to Studio Ghibli and *The Legend of Zelda*. These books are my way of sharing my passion for pop culture and food, and I use simplified culinary techniques to make sure that anyone who wants to cook these recipes can do so.

The fact that you've picked up this book tells me you're interested in Korean food or Korean dramas, and do you know what? You should be! In my ongoing quest to connect everyday cooking, street food, and food in general with pop culture, I have to admit I've rarely come across a source of inspiration as rich and powerful as K-dramas.

There isn't a single Korean drama worthy of the name that doesn't include one or more scenes of characters eating. I firmly believe that these shows are the main global showcase for Korean food, and you'll find all the classics in this book, including tteokbokki, japchae, corn dogs, kimchi, noodles, broths, soups, and braised meats. To decide which shows to include in this book, I was lucky enough to work closely with an old friend of mine, journalist and TV host Marie Palot.

Marie, a total expert on Japanese and Korean pop culture, agreed to join me on this adventure, teaching me to navigate the vibrant and prolific world of Korean dramas. Her guidance led me to create recipes inspired by *Itaewon Class*, *Hotel del Luna*, *Our Blues*, *Squid Game*, *Vincenzo*, *Hometown Cha-Cha-Cha*, *Extraordinary Attorney Woo*, and more.

The recipes are designed to be easy for you to recreate at home, introducing quintessential Korean ingredients and hearty dishes along with iconic TV series. I had a great time putting this book together, and I'm so happy I was able to do it with Marie, one of the best ambassadors of Korea and K-dramas!

Enjoy the book, bon appétit, and see you soon!

Thibaud Villanova
Gastronogeek

◖◖MEET MARIE PALOT

Thibaud and I have been friends for more than ten years now. We've met several times at various crossroads in our lives, sharing a little of ourselves for a brief moment in time. But it wasn't until 2023 that I finally got to join him on an incredible journey through his world of imagination! There aren't many people I always say yes to, and Gastronogeek is one of them. When he calls and says, "I have a project, want to talk about it?" it's already signed and sealed. Working on a cookbook that would whisk me away to an exciting world—in this case, the world of Korean television—was exactly what my bucket list had been missing.

Let me tell you a little about myself. I was born in Seoul in 1989 and arrived in France four months later. Uprooted and transplanted into a country where cooking is serious business, I began exploring my roots a little later in life. One way I did so was through Korean television, which is an excellent window into a fascinating culture. What do they eat for breakfast in the Land of Morning Freshness (and not Calm)? What is that miraculous soup that can cure you after a serious soju binge?

Korean series, or K-dramas, offer compelling visuals and a great deal of cultural insight, since *hansik* (traditional Korean food) is an integral part of a lifestyle that has been gaining in popularity for years. Korean food doesn't just feed your stomach and soul, it gives you the keys that open the doors to another world!

We have tried to recreate an alternate universe for you here, with the flavors, stories, and sense of curiosity that add color to this book. I'm extremely proud to be able to talk about a culture that belongs to me and also to someone else, the girl who might have grown up there to become a completely different Marie. I was able to connect these two sides of myself while writing this book alongside a very dear friend of mine. That might be the real magic of food—it brings people together.

If flipping through these pages makes your mouth water for distant places, then I'll consider our work a success.

Enjoy the book, enjoy your meal, and I wish you a long and happy life.

맛있게 드세요!

◖◗ CONTENTS

1

QUICK BITES

QUICK BITES

HOMESTYLE EOMUK

KOREAN-STYLE FRIED FISH STICKS

MARIE
Follow this simple recipe for a delicious plate of the ultimate comfort food!

DIFFICULTY
EASY

PREP TIME
10 MINUTES

COOK TIME
30 MINUTES

YIELD
4 SERVINGS

INGREDIENTS

1 spring onion

9 ounces cod (or other firm whitefish), deboned

7 ounces fresh calamari rings

5 ounces raw shrimp, peeled and deveined

2½ tablespoons wheat flour

2 tablespoons rice flour

1 tablespoon potato starch

2 egg whites

1½ teaspoons table salt

2 teaspoons freshly ground pepper

½ teaspoon gochujang

4 cups frying oil

EQUIPMENT

Food processor

4 wooden skewers

Cooking thermometer

Make the eomuk paste: Chop the spring onion into large pieces and transfer to a food processor. Cube the fish and calamari rings and add them to the food processor as well. Add the shrimp to the food processor along with the wheat flour, rice flour, potato starch, egg whites, salt, ground pepper, and gochujang. Process for 1 to 2 minutes to produce a smooth paste.

In a large Dutch oven (or deep fryer), heat the frying oil to 340°F. Sprinkle your work surface with flour and set a flat spatula and a few paper towels nearby. Use a soup spoon to place a large scoop of the paste onto the floured surface. With the flat spatula, form the scoop of paste into a sausage shape and lower it into the very hot oil. Fry for 5 minutes, until the fish stick is perfectly golden and floats to the surface of the oil. Use tongs to remove the fish stick carefully, without crushing it, and set it immediately on the paper towels.

Repeat until you have used up all the paste. Note that you can fry two or more fish sticks at a time.

TO PLATE
Thread two fish sticks onto each wooden skewer and serve with sauce, such as my homemade Ketchujang (see Tip on page 96)! You can also soak these fish cakes in your favorite broth.

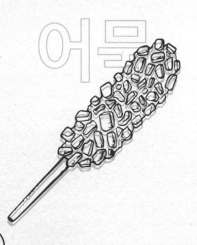

GHOSTLY MANDU

STEAMED BUNS WITH MEAT FILLING (JJINPPANG MANDU)

MARIE

Jjinppang are Korea's answer to China's bao buns—and I have a story to share about steamed buns, along with a hot tip! On my first trip to Korea, I came across a little restaurant in the traditional Insadong neighborhood of Seoul. Clouds of steam drifted through the alleyways, and the most delicious scent drew me in. They were serving all sorts of dumplings. At the time, I didn't learn the name of the restaurant, which was written in hangul. You can imagine my delight when I recognized the restaurant's sign while watching *Hotel del Luna*, seeing the protagonists walk into a Chang Hwa Dang franchise. If you're ever really hungry, I highly recommend it!

DIFFICULTY	PREP TIME	RESTING TIME	COOK TIME	YIELD
MEDIUM	30 MINUTES	ABOUT 2 HOURS	15 MINUTES	4 SERVINGS

INGREDIENTS

Dumpling dough

3 teaspoons active dry yeast

9 tablespoons warm water
(no hotter than 86°F), divided

1½ tablespoons grapeseed oil

1 teaspoon salt

3½ teaspoons sugar

2¼ cups wheat flour plus more
for working the dough

Filling

2 shallots

8 cremini mushrooms

1¾ ounces cabbage kimchi

2 stalks green garlic or 1 spring onion

½-inch piece fresh ginger

⅔ pound ground meat
(pork, beef, chicken)

Salt, for seasoning

1 teaspoon oyster sauce

Sunflower or grapeseed oil, for cooking

Dipping sauce

7 tablespoons soy sauce

2 tablespoons rice vinegar

¾ tablespoon rice syrup

1 teaspoon sesame seeds

1 small chile pepper (optional)

EQUIPMENT

Steamer basket

Parchment paper

First, prepare the dough, since it needs time to rest: To reactivate the yeast, pour the active dry yeast into a small dish and add 2 tablespoons of the warm water. Mix well and set aside for a few minutes. Pour 7 tablespoons of warm water, grapeseed oil, salt, and sugar into a mixing bowl and stir well. Add the wheat flour all at once, along with the reactivated yeast. Knead until you have a smooth ball of dough.

Cover the dough and let rise for 45 minutes to 1 hour.

Uncover the dough, punch it down, and knead it for 2 to 3 minutes. Put it back into the mixing bowl and cover again. Let rise for another 45 minutes.

Meanwhile, prepare the filling: Peel and finely chop the shallots. Mince the mushrooms. Coarsely chop the kimchi and finely chop the green garlic (or spring onion). Peel and mince the ginger. Place the ground meat into a mixing bowl, salt lightly, and fold in the shallots, mushrooms, kimchi, green garlic, ginger, and oyster sauce.

Pour a drizzle of sunflower oil into a medium frying pan and warm it over medium heat. Add the filling and stir-fry it for 5 minutes or until the meat is fully cooked. Set aside.

Punch down the dough one final time. Sprinkle your work surface with wheat flour and turn out the dough onto it. Form the dough into a thick rope, then cut into 16 equal pieces. Flatten each piece into a disc about 4 inches in diameter. Make sure that the center of the disc is thicker than the edges, which will help keep the filling contained and make the buns easier to shape. Take one disc in the palm of your hand and place 1 tablespoon of filling in the center. Fold all the edges up to meet in the middle and pinch together. Repeat for each disc of dough.

Line a steamer basket with a sheet of parchment paper. Arrange the filled buns in the basket and leave them to rest and rise for another 30 minutes.

Meanwhile, make the sauce: Stir together the soy sauce, rice vinegar, and rice syrup. Add the sesame seeds. Thinly slice the chile pepper (if using) and add it to the sauce.

Once the mandu have puffed up, they are ready to cook. Bring the water under the steamer basket to a boil, and then steam the buns for 15 minutes.

TO PLATE
Serve the mandu piping hot in their steamer basket with the dipping sauce. Take care not to burn yourself! And watch out—these are practically addictive. People have been known to eat 7 buns in a sitting!

These dumplings are absolutely to die for.

HALMEONI'S CORN DOGS

◖ *BATTERED FRIED HOT DOGS WITH HOMEMADE KETCHUP*

MARIE

When you order a hot dog in Korea, you get an American corn dog—only it might be dressed up with rice, noodles, or even Cheetos®! While TV dramas are largely responsible for the recent obsession with corn dogs (which Koreans have been eating since the 1980s), their infinite variations and affordable price are the real keys to their popularity.

DIFFICULTY
EASY

PREP TIME
10 MINUTES

COOK TIME
5 MINUTES PER CORN DOG

YIELD
4 SERVINGS

INGREDIENTS

Batter

2 cups wheat flour

1 teaspoon salt

1 teaspoon gochugaru chile powder (optional)

2 teaspoons baking powder

½ cup plus 1 tablespoon milk

1 egg

4 cups frying oil or grapeseed oil

Panko breadcrumbs, for coating

4 hot dogs

¼ cup sugar

Mustard, for drizzling

*Homemade Ketchup
(see Tip on page 96), for drizzling*

*3½ ounces mozzarella cheese
(optional, see Variation)*

EQUIPMENT

4 wooden skewers

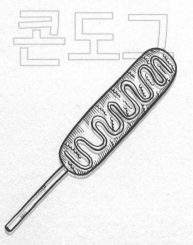

Make the batter: In a medium mixing bowl, stir together the flour, salt, gochugaru chile powder (if using), and baking powder. In a separate large mixing bowl, whisk together the milk and egg, then add in the dry ingredients. Use a silicone spatula to stir until the batter is thick and smooth. Set aside.

Pour the frying oil into a Dutch oven or deep fryer and heat it to 340°F. While the oil is heating, pour the panko breadcrumbs into a soup plate.

Insert a wooden skewer into each hot dog. Dip them one by one into the batter, then roll in the breadcrumbs to form an even coating and dip into the boiling oil for about 5 minutes.

Set a paper towel on a plate nearby. When the corn dogs are golden brown, remove them from the oil and place immediately on the paper towel to absorb the excess oil. Sprinkle lightly with sugar.

TO PLATE
Drizzle the corn dogs with mustard and homemade ketchup and serve piping hot.

VARIATION
After making the batter, cut the hot dogs into quarters and the mozzarella into pieces about 1½ inches long and the same thickness as the hot dogs. Thread the hot dog quarters onto the skewers, inserting a piece of mozzarella between every two hot dog quarters. Dip the skewers into the batter, then into the breadcrumbs. Fry for 5 minutes in the boiling oil, then set them on paper towels. Serve with mustard and homemade ketchup!

SUGGESTION
You can make these corn dogs in advance and warm them for a few minutes in an oven preheated to 400°F.

FATHER-SON EGG DROP

 SANDWICH WITH EGGS, HAM, AND CHEESE

MARIE

Egg drop sandwiches are named after the restaurant that first made them popular. They're extremely filling, and very affordable—for just a few dollars, you can pick up a quick-to-eat mega sandwich. I highly recommend ordering the Avo Holic, because it gives off the vibe that you don't bother counting your calories (otherwise known as living in denial). What's funny is that the term "egg drop" also refers to a science experiment that children do to learn about Newton's laws of motion. If I could have been eating these in middle school instead of reading Baudelaire, I never would have majored in literature, that's for sure!

DIFFICULTY	PREP TIME	COOK TIME	YIELD
EASY	15 MINUTES	5 MINUTES	1 SANDWICH

INGREDIENTS

1½ tablespoons butter

1 extra-thick (2-inch) slice sandwich bread or brioche

2 eggs

½ teaspoon gochugaru chile powder

¼ teaspoon salt

1 tablespoon store-bought or homemade Ketchujang (see Tip on page 96)

2 tablespoons cooked shredded cabbage or coleslaw

2 slices cheddar cheese

1 thick slice ham (or turkey ham)

1 tablespoon homemade Mayonnaise (see Tip on page 97)

Melt the butter over medium heat in a medium frying pan or on a griddle. Place the slice of bread in the melted butter and brown it for 2 minutes on each side. Transfer the bread to a wire rack and set aside.

Break the eggs into a bowl and add the gochugaru. Whisk very briefly; there's no need for the eggs to be frothy. Pour the eggs into the frying pan and cook for 2 minutes. Salt lightly. Use a spatula to stir the eggs and fold the edges toward the middle of the pan—you want to end up with a nice, fluffy omelet. Cut it into 2 or 3 thick pieces and set aside on a small plate.

Assemble your sandwich: Slice into the crust of the toasted bread to make the sandwich bun. Drizzle ketchujang into the bread, spoon in the cabbage or coleslaw, then add the cheddar slices. Fold the ham in half and add it into the sandwich. Finally, spoon in the fluffy omelet. Garnish with home-made mayonnaise and enjoy!

Egg drop sandwiches are definitely U-ju's favorite food! He goes out to eat them regularly, sometimes with his father, whom he adores, and sometimes with his girlfriend. Here are two recipes to celebrate some quality father-son bonding.

SANDWICH WITH EGGS, GUACAMOLE, AND FRESH AVOCADO

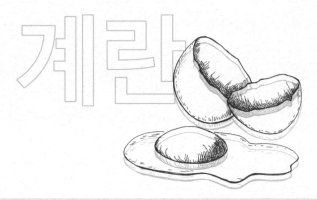

DIFFICULTY	PREP TIME	COOK TIME	YIELD
EASY	15 MINUTES	5 MINUTES	1 SANDWICH

INGREDIENTS

1½ tablespoons butter

1 extra-thick (2-inch) slice sandwich bread or brioche

Guacamole

1 ripe avocado

Juice of ½ lime

½ teaspoon sesame oil

½ teaspoon gochugaru chile powder

¼ teaspoon salt

½ clove garlic

2 eggs

½ teaspoon gochugaru chile powder

¼ teaspoon salt

1 tablespoon store-bought or homemade Ketchujang (see Tip on page 96)

Melt the butter over medium heat in a medium frying pan or on a griddle. Place the slice of bread in the melted butter and brown it for 2 minutes on each side. Transfer the bread to a wire rack and set aside.

Make the guacamole: Halve the avocado and remove the pit. Cut half the avocado into slices and coat with a few drops of lime juice to keep from oxidizing. Set aside. Scoop the other half of the avocado out into a small mixing bowl using a spoon. Pour in the sesame oil and remaining lime juice. Mash the avocado and fold in the gochugaru chile powder and salt. Peel, de-germ, and crush the garlic. Fold the crushed garlic into the mashed avocado mixture. Cover tightly with plastic wrap and set aside in the refrigerator.

Break the eggs into a bowl and add the gochugaru. Whisk very briefly; there's no need for the eggs to be frothy. Pour the eggs into the frying pan and cook for 2 minutes. Salt lightly. Use a spatula to mix the eggs and fold the edges toward the middle of the pan—you want to end up with a nice, fluffy omelet. Cut it into 2 or 3 thick pieces and set aside on a small plate.

Assemble your sandwich: Slice into the crust of the toasted bread to make the sandwich bun. Drizzle ketchujang into the bread and coat the insides. Fill generously with guacamole and the fluffy omelet. Top the sandwich with avocado slices and enjoy!

SOUPS & STEWS

02.

SOUPS & STEWS

DU-SIK AND HYE-JIN'S HANGOVER SOUP

BEEF SHORT RIB SOUP (GALBITANG)

MARIE ▸ I have a theory that the reason South Korea is known as the Land of Morning Calm is because the people there have epic hangovers. Drinking is an art, and *haejang* (recovering after a night of overindulging) is taken just as seriously. They always fight fire with fire, and fluids . . . with more fluids!

DIFFICULTY
EASY

PREP TIME
30 MINUTES

COOK TIME
4 HOURS IN THE OVEN OR 1 HOUR
30 MINUTES IN A PRESSURE COOKER

YIELD
4 SERVINGS

INGREDIENTS

1-inch piece fresh ginger

4 cloves garlic

¼ napa cabbage

1 onion

2 scallions or 1 spring onion

1¼ pounds beef short ribs or oxtail

1 marrow bone

1¾ teaspoons coarse salt

2 tablespoons gochugaru chile powder

2 tablespoons soy sauce

Sesame oil, for drizzling

8 cups water or stock (Vegetable, Chicken, Turkey, or Anchovy—see Tips on pages 92 and 93)

4 cups Cooked Rice, for serving (see Tip on page 94)

4 tablespoons cabbage or white radish kimchi, for serving

EQUIPMENT

Pressure cooker or Dutch oven

Prepare the aromatics for your soup: Smash the ginger, still in its peel, with the flat side of your knife. Repeat the process for the garlic and set both aside. Rinse the cabbage leaves and cut into large sections. Peel the onion and slice into thick rounds. Rinse and finely chop the scallions (or spring onion).

Place the beef in a large stewpot and add cold water to cover. Bring the contents of the stewpot to a gentle boil over medium-high heat and continue to cook for 10 minutes, skimming the surface regularly. Drain the meat and rinse with cold water to remove any impurities. The meat is now ready to be cooked. Here are two different methods, both simple.

IN THE OVEN
Preheat the oven to 300°F. Add the blanched meat to the Dutch oven, followed by the marrow bone, ginger, garlic, cabbage, onion, scallions, salt, gochugaru, soy sauce, and a drizzle of sesame oil. Add water (or stock) to cover. Set the Dutch oven on the stove over medium heat and bring to a boil, then turn off the heat. Cover and bake in the oven for 4 hours.

IN A PRESSURE COOKER
To the pressure cooker, add the meat, marrow bone, ginger, garlic, cabbage, onion, scallions, salt, gochugaru, soy sauce, and a drizzle of sesame oil. Add water (or stock) to cover. Cover and seal the pressure cooker following the manufacturer's instructions. Set the pressure cooker over high heat, reducing to medium heat when it first begins to hiss.

Cook for 1 hour 30 minutes.

TO PLATE
Ladle the soup into 4 large bowls, making sure to evenly distribute the ingredients. Enjoy the meltingly tender meat and rich, flavorful broth still piping hot, served with rice and white radish or cabbage kimchi. The chile and fermented flavors of the kimchi will give your soup a real kick and help you get your head back on straight.

DANBAM STEW

❮❮ *STEW WITH SILKEN TOFU, CHILE, AND VEGETABLES (SUNDUBU JJIGAE)*

◖MARIE The difference between sundubu jjigae and its close relative, kimchi jjigae, is in the texture of the tofu used. "Sun" in this case means pure— you can think of this stew as a mild(er-than-kimchi) red soup.

DIFFICULTY
EASY

PREP TIME
20 MINUTES

COOK TIME
40 MINUTES

YIELD
4 SERVINGS

INGREDIENTS

2 cloves garlic

1-inch piece fresh ginger

1¾ ounces cabbage kimchi

1½ tablespoons gochugaru chile powder

2 tablespoons Korean chile oil or vegetable oil

1 tablespoon soy sauce

1 tablespoon oyster sauce

1 teaspoon sesame oil

¼ pound ground beef

8 cups Vegetable, Beef, or Anchovy Stock (see Tips on pages 92 and 93)

8 cremini mushrooms

1 handful shimeji mushrooms (optional)

2 spring onions, minced (optional)

10½ ounces silken tofu

4 eggs

Fleur de sel, for sprinkling

Crushed black peppercorns, for sprinkling

Smash, de-germ, and finely chop the garlic. Peel the ginger, then smash and mince it as well. Chop the kimchi. Add the garlic, ginger, and kimchi to a bowl along with the gochugaru, chile oil, soy sauce, oyster sauce, and sesame oil. Stir thoroughly until thick and smooth.

Warm a Dutch oven over medium heat and pour in the mixture. Cook for 2 minutes, then add the ground beef. Stir and cook the beef for 2 minutes, using a spatula to break it up. Pour in the stock and bring to a gentle boil. Add the cremini mushrooms. Add the shimeji mushrooms and spring onions, if using. Cook for another 5 minutes before adding the silken tofu in a block. Stir well, breaking up the tofu to distribute it evenly throughout the stew. Cook for a final 20 minutes, then serve.

TO PLATE
Divide the piping hot stew between 4 soup plates or large bowls and break a raw egg over each one. Season the egg with fleur de sel and crushed peppercorns, and watch as it cooks instantly in the boiling stew!

SOUP TO BRAVE ANOTHER YEAR

RICE CAKE SOUP (TTEOKGUK)

Tteokguk soup is traditionally eaten on Seollal, in celebration of the Korean Lunar New Year. This holiday is a time when people gather with their families and honor their ancestors. Eating tteokguk, one of many must-have holiday foods, symbolizes moving up in age. That's right—everyone grows a year older on New Year's Day. But if you were planning to drown your sorrows in alcohol, you're out of luck. The meal is traditionally served with a family-friendly persimmon and ginger punch.

—MARIE

DIFFICULTY
EASY

PREP TIME
15 MINUTES

COOK TIME
20 MINUTES

YIELD
4 SERVINGS

INGREDIENTS

1 carrot

1 onion

4 heads green garlic

Grapeseed oil, for cooking

6 cups Beef or Chicken Stock (see Tips on pages 92 and 93)

2 cups Korean Anchovy Stock (see Tip on page 93)

1 tablespoon soy sauce

1 teaspoon gochujang (optional)

2 eggs

Salt, for seasoning

Toasted sesame oil, for cooking

7 ounces Tteok (rice cakes, store-bought or homemade—see recipe on page 44)

Peel the carrot and onion. Grate the carrot and thinly slice the onion. Remove the root end of the green garlic and slice each head in half lengthwise.

Pour a drizzle of grapeseed oil into a Dutch oven and warm it over medium heat. Drop the carrot, onion, and garlic heads into the hot oil and stir-fry for 2 minutes, then pour in the meat stock, anchovy stock, soy sauce, and gochujang (if using). Stir well and simmer, covered, for 15 minutes.

Crack the eggs and separate the whites from the yolks in 2 separate bowls. Salt each bowl very lightly and whisk each separately.

Use a brush or a piece of paper towel to coat a frying pan with toasted sesame oil. Warm the pan over low heat, then pour in the beaten egg yolks to make a thin omelet, similar to a crêpe. Cook covered for 2 minutes. Transfer the finished egg "crêpe" to a plate. Coat the pan with more sesame oil and repeat the process with the egg whites.

Cut both egg "crêpes" into long strips and set aside.

Gently drop the rice cakes into the broth and simmer for 5 minutes.

TO PLATE
Divide the rice cake soup between 4 bowls and arrange the strips of egg white and yolk on top. Serve right away!

NA-BI'S BIRTHDAY SOUP

◖◖ *SEAWEED SOUP WITH BEEF BROTH (MIYEOKGUK)*

○ MARIE

Seaweed soup is widely eaten by breastfeeding mothers in Korea, since the calcium and iodine stimulate lactation, among other benefits. In fact, they eat it for twenty-one days after giving birth! Because of this, children eat seaweed soup every year on their birthday to honor their mothers, who ate it when they were born. In the series, Do-hyeok makes seaweed soup and chocolate cake for Na-bi to celebrate her birthday.

DIFFICULTY
EASY

PREP TIME
15 MINUTES

COOK TIME
45 MINUTES IN
A PRESSURE COOKER
OR 3 HOURS IN
A DUTCH OVEN

YIELD
4 SERVINGS

INGREDIENTS

14 ounces beef chuck, trimmed by your butcher

1-inch piece fresh ginger

3 cloves garlic

2 onions

1 leek

1 tablespoon toasted sesame oil

8 cups water

⅔ cup soy sauce

¼ cup apple cider vinegar

1 teaspoon honey

1¼ teaspoons salt

2 teaspoons crushed black peppercorns

1¾ ounces dried miyeok (wakame seaweed)

EQUIPMENT

Pressure cooker or Dutch oven

Quarter the beef chuck, and place the pieces in a large stewpot. Add water to cover, and bring to a boil over medium-high heat. Simmer for 10 minutes, skimming the surface as necessary. Drain the blanched meat and rinse with cold water. Set aside.

Peel the ginger and use the flat side of your knife blade to smash it. Peel and smash the garlic in the same way. Peel the onions and cut each into 4 or 6 pieces.

Rinse the leek, trim the root end, and thinly slice.

Pour the toasted sesame oil into a Dutch oven or pressure cooker and warm it over medium heat. Add the beef, ginger, garlic, onions, leek, water, soy sauce, apple cider vinegar, honey, salt, and peppercorns. Stir well.

IN THE OVEN
Preheat the oven to 300°F. Set the Dutch oven on the stove and bring to a boil, then turn off the heat. Cover and place in the oven for 3 hours. Take the stew out of the oven and remove the lid. The broth should be flavorful and the meat tender. Add the dried seaweed and cook for a final 15 minutes on the stovetop over low heat, then serve.

IN A PRESSURE COOKER
Close the lid and position the valve to the correct setting. Place the pressure cooker over high heat until the valve begins to hiss. Turn the heat down to medium and let the cooker continue to hiss for 45 minutes to 1 hour. Remove from the heat, carefully release all the steam, then uncover the beef broth. Add the dried seaweed and cook for a final 15 minutes over low heat before serving.

TO PLATE
Serve the seaweed soup piping hot. Add a piece of tender beef to each bowl and enjoy right away!

OK-DONG'S STEW

◖◖ *VEGETABLE STEW WITH FERMENTED SOYBEAN PASTE (DOENJANG JJIGAE)*

◖MARIE

Despite its uninspiring name, fermented soybean paste stew is one of the tastiest dishes in Korean cuisine. Soybean paste is fermented for at least two months and up to two years and offers a wealth of benefits for the body. Doenjang jjigae is not super spicy, so choose this stew instead of kimchi jjigae, if you're sensitive. After cooking this recipe, you'll be rewarded by its intense, rich flavor. Open your mouth and close your eyes, and get ready for a pleasant surprise!

DIFFICULTY
MEDIUM

PREP TIME
20 MINUTES

COOK TIME
1 HOUR

YIELD
4 SERVINGS

INGREDIENTS

8 fresh pyogo (shiitake) mushrooms

2 cloves garlic

2 zucchini

2 russet potatoes

5½ ounces firm tofu

2 red chile peppers (optional)

1 tablespoon sunflower or grapeseed oil

Salt, for seasoning

Freshly ground pepper, for seasoning

1 tablespoon doenjang

1 tablespoon gochujang

6 cups Korean Anchovy Stock (see Tip on page 93)

4 cups Cooked Rice, for serving (see Tip on page 94)

4 tablespoons cabbage kimchi, for serving

Thinly slice the mushrooms. Peel and finely chop the garlic. Rinse the zucchini and slice in half lengthwise. Next, cut each half into ¼-inch-thick half-circles. Peel the potatoes and cut into ½-inch cubes. Cut the tofu into large cubes. Thinly slice the chile peppers (if using).

Pour the sunflower or grapeseed oil into a small Dutch oven and warm it over medium heat. Once the oil is smoking hot, add the mushrooms and stir-fry for 2 minutes, then add the zucchini and potatoes. Season lightly with salt and pepper, then add the garlic and chile pepper (if using). Add the doenjang and gochujang and stir well. Cook for 1 minute more before adding the stock and the tofu.

Simmer over low heat, covered, for 30 minutes.

TO PLATE
Serve the stew piping hot, with a small bowl of rice and cabbage kimchi.

3 PLATES TO SHARE

PLATES
TO SHARE

REPLY 1994

GOODBYE BREAKFAST

STIR-FRIED NOODLES WITH VEGETABLES (JAPCHAE)

MARIE

Koreans take eating well very seriously, so they take the time to have a hearty meal before heading off to work. Eating kimchi first thing in the morning may not be for the faint of heart, but the Korean habit of eating the same foods at breakfast and dinnertime is well-rooted in history. During the Joseon Dynasty, the royal couple ate two identical meals, called *sura*, at 10:00 a.m. and 3:00 p.m. After all, they had to be well fortified to manage any problems requiring royal attention.

DIFFICULTY	PREP TIME	RESTING TIME	COOK TIME	YIELD
EASY	20 MINUTES	1 HOUR 30 MINUTES	25 MINUTES	4 SERVINGS

INGREDIENTS

7 ounces sweet potato noodles (dangmyeon)

¼ ounce dried mogi (wood ear) mushrooms

8 pyogo (shiitake) mushrooms

1 carrot

2 spring onions

1¾ ounces soybean sprouts

3½ ounces Sesame Spinach (see recipe on page 69)

Sunflower or grapeseed oil, for cooking

2 tablespoons dark soy sauce

1 teaspoon brown sugar

Sauce

4 tablespoons dark soy sauce

2 tablespoons Korean rice vinegar

1 tablespoon plus 1 teaspoon sesame oil

1 tablespoon brown sugar

1 teaspoon sesame seeds

Soak the noodles and dried mogi mushrooms in a large quantity of cold water for 1 hour 30 minutes. Save the soaking water, which is now rich with mushroom flavor.

While the noodles and mushrooms rehydrade, make the sauce by mixing together the soy sauce, rice vinegar, sesame oil, brown sugar, and sesame seeds in a small mixing bowl.

Prepare the vegetables: Cut the pyogo and rehydrated mogi mushrooms into strips. Peel and julienne the carrot. Rinse the spring onions and separate the white from the green part. Finely chop the white part and julienne the green part. Rinse the soybean sprouts. Place the sesame spinach into a large mixing bowl.

Begin cooking: Cook each ingredient in order, separately. Pour a drizzle of sunflower (or grapeseed) oil into a medium frying pan and warm it over medium heat. Stir-fry the white part of the onions for 2 minutes. Add the mushrooms and stir-fry for 1 minute, then deglaze the pan with the soy sauce and stir in the brown sugar. Mix well and cook for another minute. Transfer the mushroom mixture to the mixing bowl and put the frying pan back over medium heat. Stir-fry the carrot pieces for 5 minutes, then add them to the bowl. Repeat the process for the green part of the onions, then the soybean sprouts.

Finally, add the rehydrated noodles to the frying pan with 3 tablespoons of mushroom water. Stir-fry for 4 minutes before adding the sauce. Stir well, cook for 1 minute more, and then add the contents of the pan to the mixing bowl.

Wearing food-safe gloves, use your hands to thoroughly mix all the ingredients together.

TO PLATE
Serve the bowl family-style on the table. Enjoy!

◖ KOREAN VEGETABLE PANCAKES (YACHAEJEON)

DIFFICULTY	PREP TIME	COOK TIME	YIELD
EASY	20 MINUTES	20 MINUTES	4 SERVINGS

INGREDIENTS

Pancake batter

2½ cups wheat flour

1 teaspoon salt

½ teaspoon gochugaru chile powder

3 eggs

1¾ cups water

1 carrot

1 zucchini

1 onion

1 small chile pepper

1½ ounces cabbage kimchi

Toasted sesame oil, for cooking

1 teaspoon salt

2 teaspoons crushed black peppercorns

Make the pancake batter: In a large mixing bowl, thoroughly combine the flour, salt, and gochugaru chile powder. Stir in the eggs. Pour in the water and continue to stir until smooth (like pancake batter). Set aside.

Prepare the vegetables: Peel and julienne the carrot. Clean and julienne the zucchini. Thinly slice the onion.

Finely chop the chile pepper. Chop the kimchi.

Pour a drizzle of toasted sesame oil into a large frying pan and warm it over medium heat. Stir-fry the carrot, zucchini, onion, chile pepper, and kimchi in the frying pan for 5 minutes. Season with salt and crushed black peppercorns.

Transfer the cooked vegetables to a plate and let cool to room temperature for 5 minutes.

When the vegetables have cooled, add them to the pancake batter and stir well.

Pour a drizzle of oil into a large frying pan and warm it over medium heat. Spoon a ladleful of vegetable pancake batter into the pan and cook for 2 minutes on each side. Your pancakes are ready when they are golden brown and cooked all the way through!

TO PLATE
Stack them into a mouthwatering pile on a plate and serve with Korean Pancake Dipping Sauce (see Tip on page 97).

NOSTALGIC TTEOKBOKKI

◖◖ *KOREAN RICE CAKES WITH SPICY SAUCE*

◊MARIE

In the series *Vincenzo*, the titular character returns to South Korea thirty years after being adopted and uprooted from his country of birth. In this version of *Lost in Translation* on steroids, he reconnects with the Korean life that he lived for just a few years through food, specifically home-cooked meals. Proust had his madeleines; for Vincenzo, it was spicy rice cakes.

DIFFICULTY
EASY

PREP TIME
30 MINUTES

COOK TIME
15 MINUTES

YIELD
4 SERVINGS

INGREDIENTS

Rice cakes

¾ cup plus 1½ tablespoons water

2½ cups rice flour (not sweet rice flour)

⅓ cup plus 1 tablespoon tapioca starch

1 teaspoon salt

Sesame oil, for drizzling and coating

4 stalks asparagus or 4 spring onions (green part only)

Sunflower oil, for stir-frying

1¼ cups Vegetable, Chicken, or Anchovy Stock (see Tips on pages 92 and 93)

7 tablespoons soy sauce

2 tablespoons gochujang

1 tablespoon sugar

First, make the rice cakes (tteok): Bring the water to a boil in a medium pot over medium heat. Add the rice flour, tapioca starch, and salt to a large mixing bowl.

Pour in the boiling water all at once and stir well with a spatula, until the dough is smooth. Set the dough on a microwave-safe dish and cover with plastic wrap. Poke a few holes in the plastic wrap and microwave for 2 minutes.

Remove the plastic wrap and knead the dough, then cover again and cook for another 2 minutes. Once the dough is heated, drizzle a little sesame oil onto your work surface and set the dough on it. Use a rolling pin or pestle to repeatedly flatten out the dough and then fold it over onto itself until it forms a smooth, even ball. Roll it into long ropes about 1 inch thick, then cut each one into sections about 2 inches long. The tteok are ready! Coat them with a little sesame oil to prevent them from sticking together, and set them aside.

Rinse the asparagus, remove the woody ends, and slice each in half length-wise. If you are using spring onions instead, rinse and thinly slice them.

Pour a drizzle of sunflower oil into a frying pan and warm it over medium heat. Drop the asparagus or onions into the hot pan and stir-fry for 2 minutes before adding the stock, soy sauce, gochujang, and sugar. Stir well until the sauce has an even consistency, then add the rice cakes. Simmer for 5 to 10 minutes over medium heat and serve immediately!

≡ JJAPAGURI EXPRESS (AKA RAM-DON)

 NOODLES WITH BLACK BEAN SAUCE, BEEF SIRLOIN, AND VEGETABLES

ᴑMARIE

In *Parasite*, when Bong Joon-ho has one of his characters garnish instant noodles with top-tier Korean beef, it sums up the very essence of the movie: two ingredients that should never have been put together. And indeed, everything starts to go pear-shaped at that exact moment in the plot.

DIFFICULTY
EASY

PREP TIME
30 MINUTES

COOK TIME
15 MINUTES

YIELD
4 SERVINGS

INGREDIENTS

1 pound beef sirloin (or Hanwoo beef filet)

Salt, for seasoning

2 young carrots

1 zucchini

4 spring onions (bulb and stem)

1-inch piece fresh ginger

1 tablespoon olive oil

4 tablespoons jjajang sauce (black bean sauce)

¾ cup to 2 cups Korean Anchovy Stock (see Tip on page 93)

Drizzle of sunflower oil

1 tablespoon oyster sauce

1 gallon water

14 ounces udon noodles

Cut the beef into 1-inch cubes. Salt lightly and set aside.

Dice the carrots, zucchini, and onion bulbs (cut into ¼-inch cubes). Finely chop the green part of the onions. Peel and mince the ginger. Set aside.

Pour the olive oil into a large skillet and warm it over medium heat. Add the jjajang sauce to the hot oil and stir-fry for 2 minutes, then mix in the carrots, zucchini, spring onions, ginger, and ¾ cup of anchovy stock. Reduce the heat to low and simmer for 5 minutes.

Pour the sunflower oil into a medium frying pan and warm it over high heat. Add the meat to the smoking hot oil. Sear for 30 seconds to form a nice brown crust, then turn and cook for an additional 1 to 3 minutes (according to your preference). Remove the meat from the pan and set on a plate topped with a paper towel to absorb excess oil, then stir into the vegetables and sauce. Pour in the oyster sauce and stir well. Feel free to add a little more anchovy stock if you prefer a runnier sauce. Keep warm over very low heat.

Bring the water to a boil in a large pot over medium-high heat, then drop in the noodles and cook until tender (following the directions on the package). Drain the noodles and add them to the other ingredients.

Serve immediately and enjoy!

NOTES

In the film *Parasite*, the character combines two different packets of instant noodles (Chapagetti® and Neoguri®) to make this dish. I decided to create a tastier version for you that requires a bit more cooking!

The dish in the film also uses Korean Hanwoo beef, an inordinately expensive beef much like Japanese Wagyu.

UNWORTHY MOTHER'S KIMCHI

 FRESH SPINACH KIMCHI

Kimchi is more than just food, it's a symbol of national pride in Korea. Koreans honor the ancient tradition and technique during kimjang, the third most important festival of the year. Communities gather to make kimchi for the winter, with more than two hundred varieties on record. Kimjang, a traditionally feminine custom that is passed down from mother to daughter, was inscribed on UNESCO's Representative List of the Intangible Cultural Heritage of Humanity in 2013. In the Korean series *Little Women*, when the mother of the three girls runs off, the inheritance she leaves them is a spectacular kimchi—and no instructions on how to make it themselves.

MARIE

DIFFICULTY
MEDIUM

PREP TIME
30 MINUTES

RESTING TIME
30 MINUTES

FERMENTATION TIME
24 HOURS MINIMUM

YIELD
2¼ POUNDS KIMCHI

INGREDIENTS

2¼ pounds spinach leaves
(or young radish greens)

½ cup salt

¾ cup plus 5 teaspoons water

¾ cup wheat flour

1 small onion

1 clove garlic

1-inch piece fresh ginger

½ Gala apple

¼ cup fish sauce

5 tablespoons gochugaru
chile powder

2½ tablespoons sugar

1 teaspoon fleur de sel

EQUIPMENT

Food processor

Prepare the spinach: Place the spinach leaves in a large bowl and sprinkle generously with the salt. Use your hands to mix the salt evenly throughout the spinach. Set aside for at least 30 minutes.

Rinse the excess salt off the spinach. Drain and press the spinach to remove all liquid. Set aside.

Prepare the marinade. Begin by making a wheat paste: Pour the water into a large saucepan and add the wheat flour. Stir well and bring to a boil over medium-high heat. Once the water boils, reduce the heat to medium and continue to cook for 10 minutes, stirring frequently. Pour the paste into a large bowl and let cool.

Peel the onion, garlic, and ginger. Add them to a food processor. Chop the apple into large pieces and add to the food processor along with the fish sauce. Process on high for 20 seconds. Scrape the resulting mixture into the bowl with the wheat paste, then stir in the gochugaru chile powder, sugar, and fleur de sel.

Thoroughly mix the spinach into the marinade bowl and then transfer it to an airtight container. Let the kimchi ferment for at least 24 hours at room temperature before moving to the refrigerator.

The kimchi is ready to eat after 24 hours. After that, it should be placed in the refrigerator, where it keeps for up to 5 months. The longer you keep it, the more it will ferment, and the more its flavors will develop.

NOTE
The very first episode of the series talks about kimchi—specifically yeolmu kimchi, which is made with young summer radishes. You can find them in Korean grocery stores. As an easier-to-find alternative, I recommend using spinach leaves.

CAPTAIN RI'S ONMYEON

 WHEAT NOODLES WITH VEGETABLES AND KOREAN BROTH

MARIE

North Korea is full of secrets. The TV series *Crash Landing on You* introduced many South Koreans to forgotten dishes like onmyeon. The noodles Captain Ri makes in his kitchen are slightly yellow, which suggests they were made with corn flour, a very common ingredient in North Korea. A simple dish has more to teach us than we realize.

DIFFICULTY
EASY

PREP TIME
15 MINUTES

COOK TIME
30 MINUTES

YIELD
4 SERVINGS

INGREDIENTS

Anchovy stock

4 cups water

2 pieces dried kelp (1½ by 2 inches each)

½ ounce dried anchovies

1 tablespoon soy sauce

1 dried pyogo (shiitake) mushroom

½-inch piece fresh ginger

Toppings

1 small zucchini

2 carrots

Vegetable oil (sunflower or olive), for cooking

Salt, for seasoning

3 eggs

4 portions wheat noodles (somyeon)

1 small chile pepper

Make the anchovy stock: Add the water, dried kelp, dried anchovies, soy sauce, dried mushroom, and ginger to a medium stewpot and bring to a boil over medium-high heat. Once the water boils, remove the kelp and reduce the heat to medium. Cover the pot and simmer while you prepare the toppings.

Prepare the toppings: Halve widthwise and then julienne the zucchini. Do the same with the carrots.

Pour a drizzle of vegetable oil into a medium frying pan and warm it over medium heat. Once the oil is hot, add the julienned zucchini to the pan. Salt lightly and stir-fry for 3 to 5 minutes without browning. Transfer to a small plate.

In the same frying pan, repeat the process for the julienned carrots, then transfer to another small plate.

In a small bowl, beat the eggs. Salt lightly. Pour a thin drizzle of oil into a frying pan and warm it over medium heat. Pour the beaten eggs into the hot oil to form a disc. Cover and cook over medium heat for 3 minutes, until the omelet is fully cooked. Transfer the omelet to a cutting board and julienne it as well.

Bring a large pot of water to a boil over medium-high heat and cook the wheat noodles until soft. Drain and rinse with cool water. Separate the noodles into 4 portions and roll each into a nest around your fingers.

Thinly slice the chile pepper.

TO PLATE

Divide the noodles between 4 bowls. Arrange a few carrot, zucchini, and omelet strips on each little pile of noodles.

Add the chile pepper and pour broth into the bowl until it almost covers the noodles.

Enjoy!

MY LOVE FROM THE STAR

CHIMAEK WITH THE GIRLS

 KOREAN FRIED CHICKEN WITH HONEY GARLIC SAUCE

© MARIE

Chimaek refers to Korean-style CHIcken and beer, "MAEKju." This dish became hugely popular in the 2010s thanks to the World Cup and the drama series *My Love from the Star*. It has since become a fixture in Korean life.

DIFFICULTY
EASY

PREP TIME
15 MINUTES

COOK TIME
20 MINUTES

YIELD
2 SERVINGS

INGREDIENTS

Sauce

3 cloves garlic

½-inch piece fresh ginger

2 tablespoons honey

2 tablespoons soy sauce

1 tablespoon rice vinegar

1 teaspoon gochujang

Chicken

4 bone-in chicken thighs

1¼ teaspoons salt

2 teaspoons freshly ground pepper

2 teaspoons gochugaru chile powder

⅔ cup potato starch

4 cups grapeseed oil

1 tablespoon white sesame seeds

EQUIPMENT

Cooking thermometer

Skimmer

Make the sauce: Peel and smash the garlic and chop it finely. Do the same with the ginger. Place the chopped ginger and garlic in a small mixing bowl, then pour the honey, soy sauce, rice vinegar, and gochujang over top. Mix well and set aside.

Prepare the chicken: Cut each thigh in half at the joint and place all the chicken pieces in a large mixing bowl. Sprinkle with salt, ground pepper, and chile powder and mix well to distribute the seasoning. Spread the potato starch out on a large rimmed plate and roll the chicken pieces in it to coat. Set the pieces aside and begin frying. The Korean two-fry method makes for juicy, extra-crispy chicken!

Pour the grapeseed oil into a deep fryer or a large Dutch oven and heat it to 300°F. Set out 2 paper towels on a plate. Gently drop the starch-coated chicken into the oil and cook for 12 to 13 minutes, until golden brown. Use a skimmer to transfer the chicken pieces to the paper towels.

Increase the temperature of the oil to 340°F and fry the chicken for another 5 minutes. Set out another 2 paper towels and transfer the perfectly cooked chicken onto them.

Pour the sauce into a large frying pan and warm over medium heat for 1 minute 30 seconds. Add the fried chicken to the pan and cook until it is thoroughly coated with sauce.

TO PLATE
Plate the pieces of chicken on a serving platter and sprinkle with white sesame seeds.

SUGGESTION
Serve this fried chicken with ice-cold beer, of course!

THE SQUAD'S PERFECT BARBECUE

 GRILLED PORK BELLY, MARINATED BEEF, AND FRIED RICE

MARIE

There's no right or wrong way to eat Korean barbecue. In fact, I'd say it's all about mixing things up. For Bok-joo, the perfect restaurant routine is just like her "awesome squad"—gargantuan and eccentric. BFN (Barbecue, Fried rice, Naengmyeon) is the ideal order for high-level athletes. Eat the meat first, fill in the gaps with fried rice, and then hydrate with a chilled soup and vegetables. The final challenge? Making it all the way through.

DIFFICULTY	PREP TIME	MARINATING TIME	COOK TIME	YIELD
MEDIUM	45 MINUTES	1 HOUR TO 12 HOURS (FOR THE BEEF)	30 MINUTES	4 SERVINGS

INGREDIENTS

Marinated beef

⅔ cup soy sauce

3½ tablespoons mijak (Korean ginger-flavored rice wine) or mirin (rice wine)

1 teaspoon gochujang

1 tablespoon honey

1 teaspoon toasted sesame oil

1 clove garlic

½-inch piece fresh ginger

½ apple or 1 Asian pear

14 ounces beef skirt steak or rib eye

Sunflower or grapeseed oil, for cooking

Grilled pork belly

2 cloves garlic

1 carrot

1 small cucumber

1 head Little Gem lettuce or a few lettuce leaves

14 ounces pork belly, trimmed and deboned by the butcher

Salt, for seasoning

Sunflower or grapeseed oil, for cooking

Ssamjang sauce, for serving

Fried rice sauce

1 tablespoon gochugaru chile powder

2 tablespoons soy sauce

1 tablespoon mirin

1 teaspoon raw sugar

1 teaspoon toasted sesame oil

2 teaspoons freshly ground pepper

Fried rice

1¾ ounces cabbage kimchi

1 clove garlic

2 spring onions

1 large sheet gim

Toasted sesame oil, for cooking

7 ounces Cooked Rice (see Tip on page 94)

EQUIPMENT

Grill pan

Make the marinated beef: Pour the soy sauce, mijak, gochujang, honey, and toasted sesame oil into a large mixing bowl. Stir well. Peel and de-germ the garlic, then chop it finely. Peel and chop the ginger. Grate the apple (or Asian pear) and add it to the marinade, along with the garlic and ginger. Set aside.

Thinly slice the beef and add it to the mixing bowl as well. Mix well to thoroughly coat the beef with marinade. Cover with plastic wrap and set aside until it is time to cook the beef. As a rule of thumb, it takes about 3 hours for a marinade to penetrate ¼ inch into a cut of meat. If you want your marinated beef to really have time to soak up the flavors, try marinating it the day before your barbecue.

Make the grilled pork belly: Cut the garlic in half and de-germ it. Peel and julienne the carrot. Rinse and julienne the cucumber. Rinse the lettuce leaves and set aside. Cut the pork belly into slices, thick or thin depending on your preference (you can also ask your butcher to do it for you). Keep in mind that thicker slices will take longer to cook, and pork must be fully cooked through. Lightly salt the slices.

Lightly coat a grill pan with sunflower or grapeseed oil. Lightly rub the surface of the grill pan with the garlic and then leave the cloves on the grill. Warm to medium heat. Arrange the slices of pork on the grill pan while it is still heating so they begin cooking on a nearly cold surface. Cook the meat for 10 to 12 minutes, turning regularly, until it is thoroughly browned and nicely grilled. Transfer the pork to a serving platter.

TO PLATE
Top a lettuce leaf with carrot, cucumber, and grilled pork. Set the ssamjang sauce nearby, then dip it and eat!

Make the fried rice sauce: Mix together the gochugaru, soy sauce, mirin, raw sugar, toasted sesame oil, and ground pepper in a small mixing bowl and set aside.

Make the fried rice: Coarsely chop the kimchi. Peel, de-germ, and finely chop the garlic. Finely chop the spring onions. Finally, use a chef's knife or a pair of scissors to cut the gim into flakes.

Pour a drizzle of toasted sesame oil into a cast-iron frying pan and warm it over medium heat. Stir-fry the chopped kimchi, garlic, and spring onion for 2 minutes before adding the cooked rice and fried rice sauce. Mix well and fry the rice for 5 minutes. Sprinkle the fried rice with gim flakes to add texture and a salty flavor that is the perfect seasoning for this dish.

Cook the beef: Lightly coat the grill pan with sunflower or grapeseed oil and warm it over high heat. Arrange the slices of marinated beef on the smoking hot grill and cook for 1 to 2 minutes on each side (to taste).

Serve immediately with the fried rice!

SUGGESTIONS
You can add meat, eggs, vegetables, or cheese to this fried rice to make it even more delicious!

To round out the squad's perfect barbecue, serve these recipes with naeng-myeon, a chilled noodle soup.

ALPHA TEAM'S SAMGYETANG

 POACHED CHICKEN WITH GINSENG AND JUJUBES

MARIE

If you walk into a Korean restaurant and say "*Yi yeol chi yeol*," you'll immediately be served a bowl of samgyetang, especially if it's hot outside. The popular expression calls for fighting fire with fire—in this case, beating the heat by eating hot food. This dish is traditionally eaten on Chobok, Jungbok, and Malbok, the three hottest days of the summer according to the lunar calendar.

DIFFICULTY
EASY

RESTING TIME
1 HOUR

PREP TIME
15 MINUTES

COOK TIME
1 HOUR

YIELD
4 SERVINGS

INGREDIENTS

¾ cup sticky rice

6 cloves garlic

2 onions

2 carrots

1 leek

1-inch piece fresh ginger

1 whole 2½-pound chicken, cleaned and prepared by the butcher

1 tablespoon salt

2½ tablespoons ground ginseng, divided

3 jujubes, fresh or dried

10 chives, chopped

2 teaspoons freshly ground pepper

Kimchi, for serving

Fleur de sel, for serving

Rinse the rice and place it in a container. Cover with water and soak for 1 hour. Drain and set aside.

Peel and de-germ the garlic. Peel and quarter the onions. Peel the carrots and cut into sections. Rinse the leek, trim the root end, and separate the green from the white part. Cut the white part of the leek into large pieces. Thinly slice the green part. Without peeling the ginger, smash it with the flat side of a chef's knife.

Lightly salt the inside of the chicken and stuff it with the white part of the leek, the sticky rice, 2 cloves of the garlic, and 1¼ tablespoons of the ground ginseng. Firmly cross the legs of the chicken to prevent the cavity from opening while cooking. Set aside.

Pour 12 cups of water into a Dutch oven and drop in the remaining 4 cloves of garlic along with the onions, carrots, leek leaves, ginger, jujubes, and the remaining 1¼ tablespoons of ginseng. Bring the water to a boil over medium-high heat and nestle the chicken into the pot, making sure the water covers it. Wait until the water returns to a boil, then reduce the heat to medium. Cover and simmer for 50 minutes to 1 hour.

TO PLATE
Sprinkle the chives and pepper on the chicken. Serve the chicken with the steaming hot broth, along with kimchi and fleur de sel.

GEU-RAMI'S KIMBAP

FRIED EGG, CABBAGE KIMCHI, AND RICE

MARIE

Kimbap has a lot going for it. It's delicious, comforting, nourishing, and most of all there are no surprises—when you're eating one, you can see exactly what's going in your mouth!

DIFFICULTY
EASY

PREP TIME
10 MINUTES

COOK TIME
3 MINUTES

YIELD
2 KIMBAPS

INGREDIENTS

Sunflower oil, for cooking

2 eggs

Salt, for seasoning

Freshly ground pepper, for seasoning

2 large sheets gim

¾ cup Cooked Rice (see Tip on page 94)

4 tablespoons cabbage kimchi

Sesame oil, for drizzling and coating

Make the fried eggs: Pour a drizzle of sunflower oil into a medium frying pan and warm it over medium heat. Break the eggs into the pan and season lightly with salt and pepper. Cook for 2 minutes, covered, then flip each egg and cook for another 1 minute, until the yolk is cooked. Transfer the fried eggs to a plate and set aside.

Assemble the kimbaps: Place a sheet of gim on your work surface. Visualize the seaweed as a square with 4 equal sections. Use your chef's knife or a pair of scissors to cut a slit in the gim from the middle of the bottom edge to the center. Scoop one quarter of the rice onto each of the lower quadrants and spread it evenly over the gim in those two sections. Place a fried egg in the upper-left quadrant of the gim and 2 tablespoons of cabbage kimchi in the top-right quadrant. Fold the lower-left section, covered with rice, over the upper-left section containing the egg. Next, fold this doubled section over the upper-right quadrant (with the kimchi), and then down over the lower-right quadrant covered with rice. Your kimbap is almost ready! Coat your knife blade with sesame oil and slice the resulting cube into 2 triangles.

Repeat the process with the remaining ingredients. Coat the finished kimbaps with sesame oil and enjoy immediately!

WOO YOUNG-WOO'S KIMBAP

SESAME RICE, BURDOCK, OMELET, GRILLED HOT DOGS, AND SPINACH

It's not so much the taste that Woo Young-woo loves about kimbaps as much as the fact that their ingredients aren't drowned in a mysterious broth. With kimbaps, Woo can see exactly what she's eating. She finds it reassuring to know there will be no surprises (which are always unpleasant). You might expect that she would develop nutritional deficiencies eating this way, but kimbaps are a fairly well-rounded food, and you can more or less put in whatever you want. Unless it's for Woo Young-woo, of course.

DIFFICULTY
MEDIUM

PREP TIME
20 MINUTES

COOK TIME
40 MINUTES

YIELD
4 KIMBAPS

INGREDIENTS

Marinated burdock

2 burdock roots

1 teaspoon sesame oil

7 tablespoons soy sauce

3 tablespoons rice vinegar

4 teaspoons soju

1 tablespoon sugar

2 hot dogs

Vegetable oil (sunflower or olive), for cooking

3 eggs

Salt, for seasoning

7 ounces spinach leaves

1 teaspoon sesame oil, plus more for assembly

1 cup Cooked Rice (see Tip on page 94)

4 large sheets dried gim

4 homemade Daikon Pickles (see Tip on page 95)

EQUIPMENT

Sushi mat

Pastry brush

Make the marinated burdock root: Peel the burdock and cut it into sticks lengthwise. Rinse and dry.

Pour the sesame oil into a medium frying pan and warm it over medium heat. Stir-fry the burdock sticks in the hot oil for 2 minutes, then add the soy sauce, rice vinegar, soju, and sugar. Stir well, cover, and continue to simmer over medium heat for 15 to 20 minutes until the burdock has absorbed as much of the liquid as possible and is tender all the way through. Set aside.

Turn the heat on the frying pan up to high. Slice the hot dogs lengthwise into 4 long sticks and add them to the pan. Sear for 20 seconds in the smoking hot pan and then set aside.

Add a drizzle of vegetable oil to the same frying pan and warm it. In a small bowl, beat the eggs and season with a pinch of salt. Pour the eggs into a pan in an even layer. You want to make a thin omelet, like a crêpe. Reduce the heat to medium and cover. Cook for 1 to 2 minutes, until the omelet is fully cooked. Transfer it to your work surface and cut it into long strips.

Rinse the spinach leaves in cool water. Prepare a large bowl of ice water. Bring a large pot of salted water to a boil over medium-high heat and drop the spinach leaves in for 20 seconds, then scoop them out and drop them into the ice water for 20 seconds. Drain and press the spinach to remove as much liquid as possible. Slice the resulting block of spinach into 4 pieces. Set aside.

Pour the teaspoon of sesame oil over the cooked rice and mix thoroughly. Divide the rice into 4 portions. For each kimbap, place 1 sheet of gim on the sushi mat. Scoop one portion of rice onto the dried seaweed and spread it over the surface, leaving about ¾ inch free along the lower edge. Along the lower edge, arrange a few strips of omelet and hot dog, one portion of spinach, a few strips of marinated burdock root, and some daikon pickles. Use the mat to roll the kimbap over itself, squeezing evenly to create a beautiful, thick roll. Coat each roll with sesame oil using a brush. Finally, coat your knife blade with sesame oil and slice the rolls into sections. Your delicious kimbaps are ready—enjoy!

MR. JANG'S STIR-FRIED NOODLES

◖◖ STIR-FRIED PORK BELLY AND BEAN SPROUTS

MARIE

A classic dish in *pojang macha* (Korean street food) is samgyupsal sukju bokkeum served just the way you like it. In fact, the dish is so popular that it's not uncommon to find it on the menu of a sit-down restaurant, accompanied by ten bottles of soju just like in a K-drama, which actually makes it an *anju* (a dish eaten with alcohol). Yes, you have a whole lot to soak up before you can hit the clubs all night long. It's very Itaewon.

DIFFICULTY
EASY

PREP TIME
10 MINUTES

COOK TIME
5 MINUTES

YIELD
4 SERVINGS

INGREDIENTS

7 ounces soybean sprouts

1 onion

4 heads green garlic

7 ounces pork belly, thinly sliced

Salt, for seasoning

Sunflower or grapeseed oil, for cooking

2 tablespoons soy sauce

1 tablespoon oyster sauce

½ teaspoon toasted sesame oil

Pinch of freshly ground pepper

1 teaspoon sesame seeds

Rinse and dry the soybean sprouts. Peel and thinly slice the onion. Remove the root end of the green garlic and slice each head in half lengthwise. Lightly salt the pork belly.

Pour a drizzle of grapeseed (or sunflower) oil into a large frying pan and warm it over high heat. Sear the slices of pork belly, frying them for 2 minutes until fully cooked. Add the soybean sprouts, onion, and green garlic to the pan and stir well. Add the soy sauce, oyster sauce, and toasted sesame oil to the hot pan while continuing to stir. Season with ground pepper and cook for another 2 minutes, stirring frequently to prevent the ingredients from sticking to the pan.

TO PLATE
Transfer to a large serving bowl to share and sprinkle with the sesame seeds.

This stir-fry is a very popular pocha order, along with a nice glass of soju!

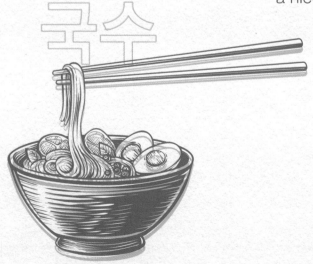

DECADENT BIBIMBAP

RICE, CABBAGE KIMCHI, SESAME SPINACH, STIR-FRIED PYOGOS, STIR-FRIED BEEF, AND BLACK BEANS

©MARIE

Apart from being the best Korean series ever aired, *Reply 1988* offers an excellent visual of what bibimbap really is. It's not a pretty stone bowl served at a restaurant with an egg nestled in the middle—not by a long shot. This is dinner as made by the harried father of two children. When his wife isn't home, he can't come up with anything better than putting all the leftover bits from the fridge into a large bowl and having the whole family eat straight from the serving dish. Armed with their spoons, they smash the picture-perfect image of people daintily picking from a table full of side dishes with their chopsticks.

DIFFICULTY
MEDIUM

PREP TIME
15 MINUTES

COOK TIME
20 MINUTES

YIELD
4 SERVINGS

INGREDIENTS

1½ cups short-grain rice

Sesame spinach

10 ounces spinach leaves

2 tablespoons soy sauce

1 teaspoon toasted sesame oil

2 teaspoons crushed black peppercorns

Salt, for seasoning

Stir-fried pyogos

6 fresh pyogo (shiitake) mushrooms

1 clove garlic

1 teaspoon sunflower or grapeseed oil

1 tablespoon soy sauce

4 eggs

3 ounces canned black beans

3½ ounces cabbage kimchi

3½ ounces marinated stir-fried beef (see page 54)

1 tablespoon store-bought or homemade Mayonnaise (see Tip on page 97)

1 tablespoon gochujang

2 tablespoons toasted sesame oil

EQUIPMENT

Pressure cooker or rice cooker

Make the rice: Rinse the rice in several changes of water and add it to the rice cooker or pressure cooker. Add 2¼ cups of water. Cook for 15 minutes until all the water has been absorbed. The rice should be well cooked, still firm but a little sticky. Transfer the rice to a dish to cool slightly.

Make the sesame spinach: Rinse the spinach. Prepare a large bowl of ice water. Bring a large pot of salted water to a boil. Blanch the spinach by cooking it in the boiling water for 30 seconds, then immediately transferring it to the ice water to cool and stop it from cooking. Coarsely chop the spinach and place it in a large mixing bowl. Pour in the soy sauce and toasted sesame oil, season with the peppercorns, and mix well to coat thoroughly and shred the spinach.

Make the stir-fried pyogos: Julienne the mushrooms. Peel and de-germ the garlic, then cut it into very fine slivers. Pour a thin drizzle of grapeseed (or sunflower) oil into a medium frying pan and warm it over medium heat. Stir-fry the mushrooms and garlic for 2 minutes, then add the soy sauce. Stir well and cook for another 30 seconds, then transfer to a bowl.

Cook the eggs: Bring a large pot of salted water to a boil, then drop in the eggs. Cook for 6 minutes if you prefer soft-boiled, or 7 minutes for almost hard-boiled eggs. While the eggs are cooking, prepare a large bowl of ice water, and drop them in when they are finished. Let the eggs cool for 5 minutes, then peel them directly in the water. Remove the eggs from the water and quarter them.

Now all you have to do is assemble everything into a deliciously decadent leftovers bibimbap! Scoop the rice into the bottom of a large bowl and spoon the black beans, cabbage kimchi, marinated beef, egg quarters, spinach, and garlic mushrooms over top. Add the mayonnaise, the gochujang, and the toasted sesame oil. Stir well and enjoy!

NOTE
Bibimbap is a dish that consists of mixing rice with other ingredients. This version is a recreation of the bibimbap made from fridge leftovers in episode 5 of the series.

MRS. KANG'S VEGETABLE PORRIDGE

◀◀ *RICE PORRIDGE (JUK) WITH SOY SAUCE–BRAISED QUAIL EGGS (GYERAN JANGJORIM)*

MARIE

Korean culture says that every physical ailment can be solved in the kitchen. And ever since the Joseon Dynasty, mothers have been making rice porridge for their children when they are on the mend. Mun-yeong has been carrying the weight of serious psychological abuse inflicted on her by her parents. When Sang-tae comes to feed her—because she is refusing to eat for herself—the result is one of the most poignant scenes ever filmed for a drama. It touches on mental health, dysfunctional families, disability, and trauma. And it shows us that sometimes, a bowl of porridge is all it takes to let it go.

DIFFICULTY
EASY

PREP TIME
20 MINUTES

COOK TIME
50 MINUTES

YIELD
1 SERVING

INGREDIENTS

Soy-braised quail eggs

6 quail eggs

1 clove garlic

⅔ cup soy sauce

1 teaspoon brown sugar

⅓ cup water

3½ tablespoons rice vinegar

Porridge

1-inch piece ginger

1 clove garlic

½ carrot

2 large white button mushrooms

Sesame oil, for cooking

3⅓ cups Vegetable Stock (see Tip on page 92)

Heaping ⅓ cup short-grain rice

Salt, for seasoning

Freshly ground pepper, for seasoning

Make the soy-braised quail eggs: Bring a pot of water to a boil over medium-high heat, drop the eggs in, and cook for 2 minutes. While the eggs are cooking, prepare a large bowl of ice water. Transfer the eggs to it when they are finished. Let the eggs cool for 5 minutes, then peel them directly in the water for easier shell removal. Set aside.

Add the garlic, soy sauce, brown sugar, water, and rice vinegar to a medium saucepan and bring to a simmer over medium-low heat. Place the peeled eggs in the saucepan and cook for 10 minutes while they absorb the simmering broth.

Prepare the rice porridge and aromatics: Use the flat side of your knife to smash the ginger and the garlic, still in its peel.

Peel the carrot and cut it into small cubes. Dice the mushrooms. Place the ginger, garlic, carrot, and mushrooms in a large saucepan, add a drizzle of sesame oil, and pour in the vegetable stock. Bring to a boil over high heat, then add the rice.

Continue to boil over high heat for 3 minutes, stirring often, then reduce the heat to low and simmer for 35 minutes.

TO PLATE

Serve your delicious porridge in a bowl with the soy-braised quail eggs! Salt and pepper, to taste.

ROYAL BEEF

SEARED HANWOO BEEF FILET WITH SESAME RICE AND EGG

MARIE

As part of their diet, Hanwoo steers are fed a special alcohol-fermented blend of barley, rice, and whole grains. This results in beef that's the perfect balance between Black Angus and highly marbled Wagyu. Apparently, including some fermented feed keeps the cattle healthy—not to mention deliciously tender and fatty. I have this mental image of a blissfully happy Korean steer, standing around in his field utterly sloshed, and it makes me feel better about eating his filets.

DIFFICULTY
EASY

PREP TIME
15 MINUTES

COOK TIME
40 MINUTES

YIELD
1 SERVING

INGREDIENTS

Salt, for seasoning

1 Hanwoo beef steak (about 1 inch thick)

Heaping ⅓ cup short-grain rice

½ teaspoon sesame oil, plus more for drizzling

1 onion

1 spring onion, green part only

2 tablespoons soy sauce

1 tablespoon rice vinegar

1 tablespoon brown sugar

Grapeseed oil, for cooking

1 fresh egg yolk

1 teaspoon sesame seeds

Freshly ground pepper, for seasoning

Lightly salt the steak on both sides and leave at room temperature for 20 minutes.

Rinse the rice 3 times in water and place in a small pot. Add enough water to cover the rice and submerge the tip of your index finger, just touching the rice, up to the first knuckle. Cover with a clear lid so you can monitor the cooking process. Bring to a gentle boil over medium heat and continue cooking over medium heat for 10 minutes. Remove the pot from the heat, but leave the lid on. Let the rice continue cooking off the heat. When it is finished, remove the lid and fluff the rice with a spatula. Drizzle a little sesame oil onto the rice and stir well, without smashing the grains. Cover with a kitchen towel and set aside.

While the rice is cooking, peel and thinly slice the onion and green part of the spring onion. Warm a medium frying pan over medium heat and pour in the ½ teaspoon of sesame oil. Add the onions and stir-fry for 1 minute before deglazing the pan with the soy sauce and rice vinegar. Sprinkle in the brown sugar and mix well. Reduce the heat to low and continue cooking for 5 minutes, then transfer the onions to a bowl.

Pour a drizzle of grapeseed oil into the same frying pan and warm it over high heat. Place the beef in the pan and sear for 30 seconds on each side. Remove from the heat.

TO PLATE
Spoon the rice into the bottom of a large serving bowl. Cover it with caramelized onions. Finally, cut the steak into nice, thick slices and fan them out attractively in the bowl. Place the egg yolk in the center. Sprinkle with sesame seeds, and season with pepper. Your royal beef is ready! Enjoy it immediately by yourself, or share it with someone who matters to you . . .

NOTE
Authentic Hanwoo beef is quite expensive, comparable to (though different from) Japan's famed Wagyu beef. You can easily find it either at a Korean grocery store or online. Otherwise, substitute rib eye, tournedos, or another thick steak.

DATE NIGHT RAMYEON?

 INSTANT NOODLES WITH VEGETABLE STOCK AND KIMCHI

♡MARIE

If you go to Korea and meet someone special, and after a romantic date, they invite you back to their place to eat ramyeon, don't expect to sit around sipping soup—your date has a different type of evening in mind. This is Korea's version of "Netflix and chill," and in fact, I strongly recommend you don't actually eat any ramyeon just before getting busy. Depending on how long you cook it, it can sit like a rock in your stomach and leave your face a little puffy the next morning. Consider yourself warned.

DIFFICULTY
EASY

PREP TIME
15 MINUTES

COOK TIME
15 MINUTES

YIELD
2 SERVINGS

INGREDIENTS

3½ ounces cabbage or spinach kimchi

4 handfuls fresh spinach leaves

4 heads green garlic

1 onion

2 cloves garlic

½-inch piece fresh ginger

4 pyogo (shiitake) mushrooms

1 tablespoon sunflower or grapeseed oil

2 tablespoons soy sauce

1 tablespoon rice vinegar

4 cups stock (Vegetable, Beef, Chicken, or Anchovy—see Tips on pages 92 and 93)

2 portions instant noodles

Coarsely chop the kimchi and spinach. Slice the green garlic in half. Peel and thinly slice the onion. Peel and chop the garlic and ginger. Slice the mushrooms into strips.

Pour the oil into a Dutch oven and warm it over medium heat. Add the onion and sauté for 2 minutes, then add the garlic, ginger, spinach, green garlic, mushrooms, and kimchi. Stir well and cook the mixture for 5 minutes, then deglaze with the soy sauce and rice vinegar. Mix thoroughly and stir in the stock. Bring to a gentle boil and cook for 8 minutes, covered.

Meanwhile, cook the noodles according to the instructions on the package. Once the noodles have reached your preferred texture, drain them and divide between 2 bowls.

TO PLATE
Pour the kimchi broth and vegetables over the bowls of noodles and enjoy your hot . . . soup!

Ramyeon makes a cameo in many K-dramas—hardly surprising, since it's an everyday staple in Korea. But you should know that eating ramyeon together on a date might be considered foreplay. Which Lee is very flustered to find out . . .

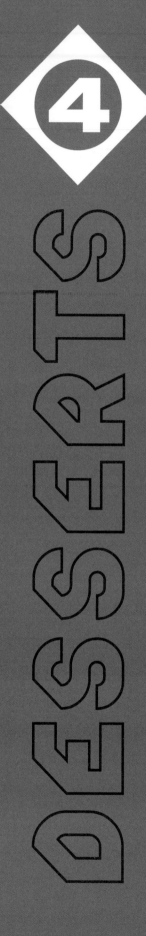

4

DESSERTS

DESSERTS

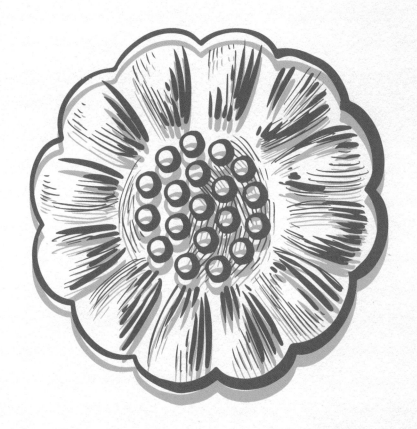

TELLTALE BUNGEO-PPANG

CRISPY WAFFLES WITH RED BEAN FILLING (ANKO)

MARIE

Bungeo-ppang and ingeo-ppang are comfort food for the cold winter months in Korea. While Vincenzo has his own unique trick for telling the two apart, there is a much easier way. Just remember that you can't see what's inside a bungeo-ppang at all, but the sweeter ingeo-ppang lets you see through to the filling.

DIFFICULTY
EASY

PREP TIME
10 MINUTES

RESTING TIME
1 HOUR

COOK TIME
4 MINUTES PER WAFFLE

YIELD
8 WAFFLES

INGREDIENTS

Bungeo-ppang batter

3½ teaspoons brown rice syrup or 2¼ tablespoons brown sugar

2 eggs

3 tablespoons water

⅔ cup milk

2½ tablespoons neutral vegetable oil or 1½ tablespoons melted butter, plus more for greasing

1 cup plus 3 tablespoons bread flour

1 teaspoon baking powder

1 teaspoon salt

Filling

4 ounces store-bought or homemade Danpat (see Tip on page 95) or 4 ounces Nocciolata® or 4 ounces chestnut cream

EQUIPMENT

Fish-shape waffle iron

Make the bungeo-ppang batter: Pour the brown rice syrup or brown sugar into a large mixing bowl, then add the eggs. Whisk vigorously, then mix in the water, milk, and oil or butter. In a separate medium mixing bowl, combine the flour, baking powder, and salt. Mix the dry ingredients into the wet ingredients, continuing to whisk until there are no lumps. Set aside.

Preheat your waffle iron over medium heat. The key to this recipe is patience! First, grease the mold with a brush or a piece of paper towel soaked in oil. Then ladle a small amount of waffle batter into the mold, taking care not to fill it to the brim, and place 1 teaspoon of danpat (or your chosen filling) in the center. Pour in more batter and close the waffle iron.

Cook for 2 to 2½ minutes, then grip the waffle iron firmly shut and flip it over. Cook for another 1½ minutes, then remove your waffle from the mold and set it on a wire rack.

Continue to make bungeo-ppang until you have used up all the batter.

Serve right away!

THE DALGONA CHALLENGE

 HONEYCOMB CANDY

MARIE

Dalgona means "it's sweet." These candies, also known as ppopgi or gukja, first made their appearance in the 1960s and 1970s around Korean schools. The simple recipe mixes melted white sugar with baking soda to make it frothy, and a shape is imprinted onto each candy. Traditionally, if you managed to eat the candy without breaking the shape, you won a free dalgona. Of course, it's not easy!

DIFFICULTY
EASY

PREP TIME
2 MINUTES

COOK TIME
15 MINUTES

YIELD
4 DALGONAS

INGREDIENTS

4 tablespoons white sugar
½ teaspoon baking soda
Grapeseed oil, for greasing

EQUIPMENT

Silicone baking mat
Cookie cutter in the shape of a circle, triangle, star, or umbrella
Circular press (optional)

Pour the sugar into a small saucepan and warm it over low heat. Use wooden chopsticks to stir the sugar continuously for 5 to 10 minutes. You are making caramel, which can take some time. When the sugar has completely melted into liquid, stir in the baking soda. Continue to cook for 2 minutes, still stirring, until the mixture is smooth and even.

Pour 4 mounds of the melted sugar mixture onto a silicone baking mat, making sure to leave space between them. Grease the cookie cutter and circular press (or the bottom of a glass). Press each mound into a disc and use the cookie cutter to imprint your chosen shape.

Let the candies cool before serving. If you really want to get the shape out without breaking it, try using a needle!

It's much easier to make these candies than it is to break the shape out of the center, especially if your life is on the line!

YOON SE-RI'S NURUNGJI

◖◖ *SWEET SCORCHED RICE*

MARIE

Originally used as a home remedy for stomach ailments in the seventeenth century, nurungji metamorphosed into a dessert in the 1970s. "Nureun" refers to the yellowish or reddish scorched state of the rice in the bottom of the cooking pot. Apparently, even in a K-drama, an oldie can be a goodie.

DIFFICULTY
EASY

PREP TIME
5 MINUTES

COOK TIME
5 MINUTES

YIELD
4 SERVINGS

INGREDIENTS

Sunflower or grapeseed oil, for cooking

7 ounces Cooked Rice (see Tip on page 94)

2½ tablespoons sugar

Pour a thin drizzle of oil into a large frying pan and warm it over medium heat. Spoon little mounds of cooked rice over the entire surface of the pan, then press them down with a spatula to create a thin, even layer. Once the rice cake is golden brown, flip it and cook for 1 minute on the other side before transferring to a plate.

Repeat until you have used up all the rice. Let the rice cakes cool, then break them and dip in sugar to eat.

SUGGESTION
These rice cakes can be stored for several days in an airtight container.

Making this munchable crunchy rice couldn't be easier!

SOOTHING YAKGWAS

TRADITIONAL DEEP-FRIED GINGER COOKIES

♡ MARIE

Yakgwas are among the oldest sweets in Korea, dating all the way back to the Three Kingdoms period (57 BCE to 668 CE)! Over the centuries, they became so popular that some kings forbade people from making them, because it would result in flour, oil, or honey shortages. The cakes are still considered a health remedy, and they hit the perfect sweet note to round out a good meal.

DIFFICULTY
MEDIUM

PREP TIME
20 MINUTES

RESTING TIME
13 HOURS

COOK TIME
10 MINUTES

YIELD
20 COOKIES

INGREDIENTS

Cookie dough

1½ cups plus 1 tablespoon wheat flour

½ cup sticky rice flour

⅓ cup toasted sesame oil, plus more for forming the dough

⅓ cup honey

½ cup plus 4 teaspoons soju

4 cups neutral oil (grapeseed or sunflower), plus more for greasing

Syrup

1-inch piece fresh ginger

½ cup honey

½ cup rice syrup

½ teaspoon salt

1½ teaspoons ground cinnamon

EQUIPMENT

Yakgwa mold
Cooking thermometer

Make the cookie dough: Sift the wheat flour and sticky rice flour into a large mixing bowl. Pour the toasted sesame oil over top and rub it into the flour with your fingers to create a sandy mixture with a light sesame scent. Sift the flour mixture again, pressing with a spatula if necessary.

In a separate medium mixing bowl, stir together the honey and soju to thoroughly combine. Pour the honey-soju mixture over the flour and knead for 8 minutes to form a smooth dough. Shape it into a disc, cover with plastic wrap, and refrigerate for 30 minutes.

Meanwhile, make the syrup: Peel the ginger and smash it with the flat side of your knife. Set aside.

Combine the honey, rice syrup, salt, cinnamon, and ginger in a small saucepan. Bring to a boil over high heat, then reduce the heat to medium. Continue cooking for 5 minutes, stirring constantly with a wooden spatula. Remove the saucepan from the heat and set aside the honey-ginger syrup.

Take the cookie dough out of the refrigerator. Divide it into 20 equal pieces. Pour a drop of toasted sesame oil into your palm and spread it over your hands to coat. Roll each piece of dough into a ball.

Grease a yakgwa mold with neutral oil and press each dough ball into the mold to make the cookie shapes.

Pour the 4 cups of oil into a pot or deep fryer. Heat the oil to 320°F, then drop the cookies in one at a time. Fry the cookies for 2 to 3 minutes and then flip to brown evenly on both sides. Continue frying until the cookies are golden brown all over, then transfer to a paper towel–lined plate.

Cover and set aside for 30 minutes. Arrange the cooled cookies in a dish. Pour the syrup over them and let them soak for at least 12 hours before serving!

Yakgwas are a very ancient and extremely popular traditional Korean pastry. Their texture and honeyed flavor give them a sweetness that is thought to soothe the heart and mind.

BANANA MILK

 BANANA SMOOTHIE

(MARIE)

Banana milk, or banana uyu, is the first thing you should buy at a convenience store to make sure that you're not just dreaming and you really are in Korea. It's kind of like buying tuna mayo onigiri at a 7-Eleven in Tokyo. Since 1974, Koreans have been bombarded with a campaign encouraging them to drink milk—but at first, it was a complete flop. Then someone thought to add a few drops of banana flavoring and vanilla, and suddenly they became a nation of milk addicts! Estimates suggest that billions of bottles of banana milk, shaped like traditional Korean jars, have been sold since the 1970s. Personally, I drink about ten a day whenever I'm in Korea.

DIFFICULTY
EASY

PREP TIME
5 MINUTES

YIELD
1 SERVING

INGREDIENTS

1 ripe banana

1 tablespoon sweetened condensed milk

1 tablespoon rice syrup

1 cup whole milk, or soy or almond milk

A few ice cubes

EQUIPMENT

Blender

Peel the banana and cut into pieces. Add the banana to a mixing bowl and smash it using a fork or potato masher.

Stir in the sweetened condensed milk and the rice syrup.

Scrape the mixture into the blender and add the milk and ice cubes.

Blend on high for 30 seconds, or until frothy and smooth, and serve cold!

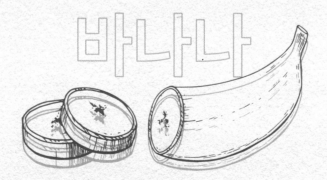

EUN-JAE'S HOMEMADE MARMALADE

YUJA HONEY MARMALADE

MARIE

When a head cold starts to creep down your throat into your chest, try this effective remedy that all Koreans use: yuja cha, a tea made from yuja-cheong (yuja plus sugar) diluted in hot water. It's sweet, fruity, comforting, and seems to coat your burning throat with a soothing layer of honey.

DIFFICULTY
EASY

PREP TIME
10 MINUTES

RESTING TIME
30 MINUTES PLUS 12 HOURS

YIELD
TWO 1-LITER JARS

INGREDIENTS

8 Korean yuja (yuzu) fruits, or 8 organic lemons

2¼ pounds jam sugar, plus a little more for sprinkling

1 tablespoon honey

EQUIPMENT

Two 1-liter jars

Scrub the fruits under a thin stream of warm water. Cut them in half and remove the seeds, then cut the entire fruit into thin slices, including the zest, pith, and pulp. Place the slices in a large mixing bowl.

Add the 2¼ pounds of jam sugar and the honey all at once. Mix well to coat the fruit with sugar. Set aside for 30 minutes while the sugar draws the juice out of the fruit.

Scoop the mixture into 2 jars. Use the remaining sugar to sprinkle the surface of the contents of each jar, forming a protective layer, then close the jars. Leave at room temperature for at least 12 hours before using or moving to the refrigerator for longer storage.

NOTES

We suggest using organic yuzu since the rind is consumed in this recipe.

You can use this marmalade to make tea: Simply add 1 tablespoon of it to 1 cup of simmering water. It's also delicious on toast!

VARIATION

Try including pieces of fresh ginger in your marmalade for a more complex flavor.

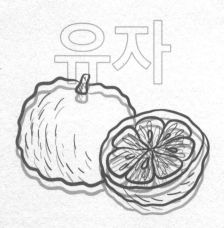

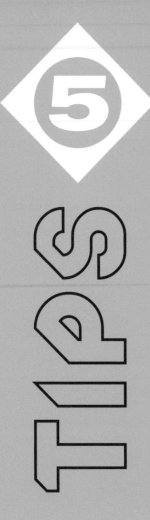

5

TIPS

TIPS

⫴ VEGETABLE STOCK

PREP TIME	COOK TIME	RESTING TIME	YIELD
5 MINUTES	2 HOURS	30 MINUTES	8 CUPS OF STOCK

INGREDIENTS

4 carrots

1 leek, white part only

½ stalk celery

1 onion

1 shallot

1 bouquet garni (green part of 1 leek, 4 stems parsley, 1 stalk fennel, 1 bay leaf, 1 sprig thyme)

8 cups water

⅔ cup white wine

1 star anise

3 cardamom pods

Dice the carrots. Cut the leek, celery, onion, and shallot into small pieces.

Place the carrots, leek, celery, onion, shallot, bouquet garni, water, white wine, star anise, and cardamom pods in a stewpot and simmer over medium-low heat for 2 hours, covered.

Remove stock from heat and let cool for 30 minutes, then strain.

⫴ CHICKEN OR TURKEY STOCK

PREP TIME	COOK TIME	YIELD
20 MINUTES	4 HOURS 15 MINUTES	8 CUPS OF STOCK

INGREDIENTS

4½ pound chicken or turkey carcass

7 tablespoons grapeseed oil

3½ tablespoons unsalted butter

1 clove garlic, chopped

2 shallots, chopped

8 cups water

1 bouquet garni (thyme and bay leaf tied in a green leek leaf)

1 sprig rosemary

2 juniper berries

Pinch of crushed peppercorns

Crush the turkey or chicken carcass and sauté it in an oven-safe stewpot with the grapeseed oil and butter. Stir and cook over medium heat until the carcass turns golden brown. Remove it from the pot and set aside.

Preheat the oven to 300°F. Skim off the fat from the cooking pot, but leave the cooking juices in the pot. Simmer the chopped garlic and shallots in the cooking juices for no longer than 5 minutes over medium heat. Remove from the heat.

Pour in the water, add the bouquet garni, and cook in the oven for 3½ hours. Add the rosemary, juniper berries, and peppercorns to the stewpot, then return the pot to the oven for another 30 minutes. After 4 hours total in the oven, strain the contents of the stewpot, saving only the liquid.

⦙⦙⦙ BEEF STOCK

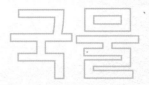

PREP TIME	COOK TIME	RESTING TIME	YIELD
20 MINUTES	4 HOURS 15 MINUTES	SEVERAL HOURS	8 CUPS OF STOCK

INGREDIENTS

1 pound beef (bottom round or chuck)

Salt, for seasoning

1 clove garlic

2 carrots

2 onions

7 tablespoons grapeseed oil

3½ tablespoons unsalted butter

8 cups water

1 bouquet garni (thyme and bay leaf tied in a green leek leaf)

1 sprig rosemary

2 juniper berries

Pinch of crushed peppercorns

Preheat the oven to 300°F. Cut the beef into large cubes. Salt lightly and set aside. Use the flat side of your knife blade to smash the garlic. Rinse and dry the carrots; do not peel. Cut into large pieces. Quarter the onions with their skins still on. Pour the grapeseed oil and butter into a Dutch oven and warm over medium heat. Once the Dutch oven is hot, sauté the garlic, carrots, and onions. Turn up the heat to medium-high and sear the beef on all sides. Once the beef is nicely browned, add the water, bouquet garni, rosemary, juniper berries, and peppercorns. Stir well and cover.

Cook in the oven for 4 hours.

After the stock is done, filter it through a fine-mesh strainer, retaining the liquid an discarding the solids. Let cool before placing the stock in the refrigerator.

After several hours, skim off and discard the layer of fat that should have formed on top of the broth.

⦙⦙⦙ KOREAN ANCHOVY STOCK

PREP TIME	COOK TIME	YIELD
10 MINUTES	10 MINUTES	4 CUPS OF STOCK

INGREDIENTS

4 cups water

2 pieces dried kelp (1½ by 2 inches each)

½ ounce dried anchovies

1 tablespoon soy sauce

1 dried pyogo (shiitake) mushroom

½-inch piece fresh ginger

Add the water, dried kelp, dried anchovies, soy sauce, dried mushroom, and ginger to a medium saucepan and bring to a boil over high heat. Once the water boils, remove the kelp and reduce the heat to medium.

Cover the pot and simmer for ten minutes.

||| COOKED RICE

PREP TIME	COOK TIME	RESTING TIME	YIELD
5 MINUTES	20 MINUTES	SEVERAL HOURS	1 CUP COOKED RICE

INGREDIENTS

Heaping ⅓ cup short-grain rice per serving

Drizzle of sesame oil

Rinse the rice in 3 changes of water and place in a small pot. Add enough water to cover the rice and submerge the tip of your index finger, just touching the rice, up to the first knuckle. Cover with a clear lid so you can monitor the cooking process. Bring to a gentle boil over medium heat and then continue cooking for 10 minutes.

Remove the pot from the heat, but leave the lid on to let the rice continue cooking off the heat. When it is finished, remove the lid and fluff the rice with a spatula. Drizzle a little sesame oil onto the rice and stir well, but without smashing the grains. Cover with a kitchen towel and set aside.

⦙⦙⦙ DANPAT PASTE (ANKO)

PREP TIME	COOK TIME	RESTING TIME
10 MINUTES	1 HOUR 15 MINUTES	2 HOURS

INGREDIENTS

7 ounces adzuki beans

3 cups mineral water

¾ cup plus 2 tablespoons sugar

Pinch of salt

Soak the adzuki beans for 2 hours in a bowl of cold water.

Drain and transfer to a medium saucepan. Add water to cover, and then bring to a gentle boil. Cook for 5 minutes. Then drain the beans and repeat this step with a fresh pot of water.

By this time, the beans should have lost any bitterness. Pour the mineral water into the saucepan and add the beans back in. Cook at a gentle boil over medium heat for 50 minutes to 1 hour, until they are soft all the way through.

Remove from the heat and leave the beans to soak in the hot water for another 10 minutes.

Drain off about ⅓ of the cooking water, and add the sugar and pinch of salt. Turn the heat back to medium and simmer for 15 to 20 minutes, stirring frequently. You want the mixture to reduce until you have a nice mashed consistency, not too runny but still slightly syrupy. Your red bean paste is ready!

⦙⦙⦙ DAIKON PICKLES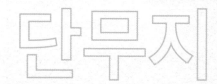

PREP TIME	COOK TIME	RESTING TIME	YIELD
10 MINUTES	5 MINUTES	1 HOUR	TWO 1-LITER JARS

INGREDIENTS

2 daikon radishes (about 7 ounces)

1-inch piece fresh ginger

1 teaspoon turmeric

3¾ cups water

2½ cups white vinegar

1¼ cups sugar

EQUIPMENT

Two 1-liter jars

First, peel the daikon radishes and cut them into sticks or rounds. Peel and chop the ginger. Stir together the daikon radishes, ginger, and turmeric in a medium mixing bowl.

Divide the mixture into airtight jars. Set aside.

Combine the water, white vinegar, and sugar in a medium saucepan. Bring to a boil over medium-high heat and then pour the hot pickling liquid over the daikon mixture in the jars. Let cool, then seal the jars and store in the refrigerator.

You can eat the daikon pickles right away or store them in the refrigerator for up to several weeks.

⠿ KETCHUP

PREP TIME	COOK TIME	YIELD	EQUIPMENT
10 MINUTES	30 MINUTES	1 SMALL BOTTLE	IMMERSION BLENDER MESH STRAINER

INGREDIENTS

1 clove garlic

1 red onion

6 very ripe tomatoes

2 tablespoons olive oil

2 pinches ground ginger

2 pinches ground cumin

2 tablespoons tomato paste

1½ tablespoons brown sugar

¼ cup plus 3 tablespoons red wine vinegar

Salt, for seasoning

Freshly ground pepper, for seasoning

Peel and finely chop the garlic and onion. Set aside. Blanch and peel the tomatoes, then cut into large pieces. Set aside.

In a small saucepan, warm the olive oil over medium heat. Add the garlic and onion and sauté for 3 minutes. Sprinkle with ground ginger and cumin and stir in the tomato paste thoroughly with a wooden spoon. Stir in the chopped tomatoes, then add the brown sugar. Bring the mixture to a boil and simmer over low heat for 15 minutes, covered, then remove the lid and cook for another 10 minutes to reduce the liquid. Stir in the red wine vinegar, and salt and ground pepper to taste.

Finally, use an immersion blender to blend the mixture for 2 minutes. Pour it through a conical-mesh strainer, reserving the ketchup and discarding any solids. Let the ketchup cool before bottling.

⠇ KETCHUJANG

PREP TIME	YIELD
2 MINUTES	1 SMALL BOTTLE

INGREDIENTS

1 small bottle homemade Ketchup (see above)

1 to 2 tablespoons gochujang

½ teaspoon sesame oil

Mix together the ketchup, gochujang, and sesame oil in a medium mixing bowl. Note: Ketchujang is spicy! Feel free to adjust the amount of gochujang to your own taste.

This recipe makes a ketchup with Korean flavors that I love to make when I'm cooking fried chicken or grilling meat.

⦚ MAYONNAISE

PREP TIME	YIELD
7 MINUTES	4 SERVINGS

INGREDIENTS

1 extra-fresh organic egg yolk

1 tablespoon mustard

¾ cup plus 1½ tablespoons vegetable oil

Salt, for seasoning

Before you start: Note that all the ingredients must be at the same temperature to emulsify.

Add the egg yolk and mustard to a medium mixing bowl. Use a fork or whisk to stir vigorously while drizzling in the oil in a constant thin stream. Continue stirring until the mixture transforms into mayonnaise. Salt to taste.

Store your mayonnaise in the refrigerator, covering the surface with plastic wrap to prevent a skin from forming.

VARIATION: SPICY MAYONNAISE

For spicy mayonnaise, quickly stir in ½ to 1 teaspoon of gochujang once the mayonnaise has emulsified.

⦚ KOREAN PANCAKE DIPPING SAUCE

PREP TIME	YIELD
5 MINUTES	1 CUP SAUCE

INGREDIENTS

1 tablespoon gochujang

1 teaspoon doenjang

1 teaspoon rice syrup

⅔ cup soy sauce

2½ tablespoons soju

2½ tablespoons water

1 teaspoon sesame seeds

Place the gochujang and doenjang in a small mixing bowl. Stir well, then add the rice syrup.

Mix in the soy sauce, then the soju, and finally the water and sesame seeds.

6

KOREAN INGREDIENTS

KOREAN INGREDIENTS

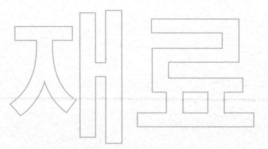

❝ *HERE IS A LIST OF THE INGREDIENTS YOU MUST HAVE ON HAND IF YOU WANT TO COOK KOREAN FOOD!*

ASIAN PEAR
I love this fruit, which looks like an apple and can be used the same way apples are in cooking. It is delicious in a pie or a crumble; its flavor is delicate and its juice refreshing.

CHUNJANG
Chunjang is a fermented black bean paste with a balanced sweet and savory taste. While it is traditionally black in color, different brands may be more or less fermented and appear lighter or darker. Chunjang is one of the main ingredients in the sauce for jajangmyeon.

CITRUS
Citrus fruits are very common in Korean cooking. The zest and juice of yuja and combawa, for example, are used in condiments. They can also be made into marmalade and used to make tea and hot beverages.

DASIMA
Known as kombu in Japan, dasima (in Korean) is a dried green or black kelp used to make stock. It is one of the traditional ingredients in Korean cooking.

DOENJANG
Alongside gochujang and ssamjang, doenjang is one of the three most commonly used condiments in Korean cooking. This soybean paste, similar to Japanese miso, is the result of a long fermentation process. It has a strong flavor.

DRIED ANCHOVIES
Along with dasima (kelp), anchovies are one of the ingredients in traditional Korean broth. When simmered with seaweed in water, they give the broth its characteristic subtle fish flavor.

DRIED JUJUBES

Also known as red dates or Chinese dates, jujubes are fruits used to add a refreshing, fruity flavor to broths and sauces.

DRIED SEAWEED

In general, seaweed is used to add flavor, color, and character to a dish.

GARLIC

This edible plant is used to flavor stir-fried vegetables, infused into oils and stocks, and rubbed on toast. Garlic offers many health benefits and a pungent flavor.

GIM

This dried seaweed, similar to Japanese nori, is used to make recipes such as kimbap (Korean rice rolls). It adds flavor to broths and is used as a condiment on many dishes.

GINGER

Dried ground ginger is used around the globe to add a hint of spice and a refreshing flavor to food. Ginger root is also smashed or chopped and used fresh, for ten times the flavor and intensity.

청정원
essential

남해안산
청정다시마

KELP

종가집
JONGGA

갓 뽑은 듯 쫀득하고 부드러운
순쌀 떡볶이떡
Rice Cake (Tubular Type)

GMP
건강기능식품

大韓民國特産品

高麗
人蔘茶

KOREAN
GINSENG
TEA

NET WT. 3g×30포

PEPPER (COARSE)
ORE (GROS)

복음용
짜장
BLACK BEAN PASTE

엄마가 해준 그 맛 그대로
진미울리지널
춘장
SINCE 1957

Mr.Jin

300 g (530 Kcal)

KOREAN INGREDIENTS

GINSENG
This root is commonly used in Asian food, including Korean. It offers many health benefits, whether added to stock or used in a traditional samgyetang.

GOCHUGARU
Powder or flakes of dried, crushed chile peppers. It is used in the same way as red chile flakes, as a seasoning or condiment.

GOCHUJANG
This is the quintessential Korean condiment! It is a fermented chile paste made with wheat germ, sticky rice flour, and meju, a fermented soybean paste. Its flavor is intense, spicy, and slightly sweet.

MUSHROOMS
Mushrooms are very common in Asian food, particularly Korean. Korea has an ideal climate for growing and developing mushrooms like saesongyi (king oysters). Pyogos (shiitakes) are also used fresh in salads and stir-fries, and dried in soups and broths.

NOODLES
Korean recipes use several types of noodles, including dangmyeon (sweet potato vermicelli) and somyeon (thin wheat noodles). They are served in broth, with stews, and in chilled soups.

RICE (BAP)
Rice is a staple on Korean tables. It can be steamed and eaten plain, stir-fried, rolled into kimbaps, or mixed into stews.

RICE VINEGAR

Korean or Japanese rice vinegar is mild and flavorful. It is used as a base for sauces and vinaigrettes and as a flavoring for kimbap rice and meat marinades.

SESAME OIL

Sesame oil is the single most frequently used ingredient in Korean cooking. You will find yourself reaching for it when making rice, preparing many sauces, seasoning meat, or mixing up marinades.

SOJU

This Korean spirit can be made from rice, potatoes, or wheat. It is used in cooking to deglaze a pan, add flavor to sauces and stocks, and marinate meats.

SSAMJANG

This fermented condiment is a mixture of gochujang and doenjang. It is used as a sauce base and traditionally served with grilled meats.

TTEOK

Tteok are sticky rice cakes that have been kneaded and steamed. They come in sticks or cylinder shapes and may be served in desserts or in spicy, savory dishes like tteokbokki.

▚ INGREDIENT INDEX

INGREDIENT INDEX

▌▌▌ INGREDIENT INDEX

INGREDIENT INDEX

NOTES

ACKNOWLEDGMENTS

You've come to the end of the book—I hope you liked it!

Thank you to Bérengère and to my son, Henri. Béren, thank you for encouraging me to believe in this project so long ago, thank you for helping me breathe life into it, and thank you for setting such high standards as artistic director and keeping the project on track. Finally, thank you for insisting that we spend an evening watching *Hometown Cha-Cha-Cha*, which is what made me want to dive into Korean cooking! Henri, I can't wait for us to cook all these recipes together and for you to savor the rich, spicy flavors!

Thank you to my parents and my sister for your tireless support, love, and confidence. Dad, the more I think about it, the more I realize that I owe my passion for cooking to one of your apple pies. Simple, humble, and fantastic, seasoned with an expert hand and with the love you have always had for us. Thank you for that spark—thank you for everything.

Thank you to Marie for trusting me and agreeing to take part in this fabulous project! I want to take this opportunity to thank you for your wise counsel over all these years, and for your friendship, which means a lot to me. My words may be clumsy, but they come from the heart.

Thank you, Julien, for the design and the inspired graphics work you did for this book! As always, you gave us the very best, and I'm grateful.

Thank you to Mehdiya Kerairia and Nicolas for their hard work on styling and photography. Yet again, you have succeeded in bringing my creations to life—thank you.

Thank you to my team, particularly Baptiste, who is my right hand in everything, and whose hard work and eye for detail make my creative work better.

Thank you to everyone who lent me their time, advice, and other items.

Thank you to Catherine and Anne with Hachette Heroes, you know how much I love working with you, and I hope we'll keep on doing it for many years!

Thank you to everyone at Hachette Heroes who will put this cookbook into your hands and make sure it gets the attention it deserves.

I couldn't let you close this book without a heartfelt thank you to my dear community—readers, viewers, fans who have been with me from the start and silent observers alike. Thank you. Thank you. Thank you. THANK YOU.

Thibaud Villanova
Gastronogeek

Let me begin by thanking my host, without whom I would not be here today: Thank you, Thibaud, for inviting me to work on this book. I am very proud of what we've created. Your trust and friendship mean so much to me, and I am extremely grateful to have known you for so many years.

Thank you to my family for your unfailing support, and to my parents, who are extraordinary guides in this life. To my big brother, my role model and ally. I love you all more than anything.

My partner, Fabien, who puts fresh wings on my back day after day, encouraging me to take flight and be happy. I am inspired every day by the example of his success and his humility. Our son, Noah, that perfect and marvelous child who breathed new life into me in indescribable ways, like a perpetual breeze constantly filling my sails and moving me toward new horizons. Thank you, my son, for giving me the most meaningful job of my life—being your mother. I'll make you proud.

Thank you to everyone who had confidence in me, without whom I would never have found my way to the platforms that carry my voice, from the *Nyûsu Show* and *Zine! Zine!* to RTL9 and my adventures on Twitch.

Thank you to all my friends who have always supported me, even in an industry where competition is fierce and friendships are fragile. Particularly my little brother, Louis San, whose advice I rely on, and Anaïs Marion and Dracony, my chosen family. My Korean language classmates, Victor Yellowtotor and Carine, my right hand Pierre, Noemie, and everyone who helps me grow and learn every day.

Finally, I want to thank all of you who have followed me for years. You give me so much strength. Alyson, Alexandre, Chloé, Emilie, and all the others who have never stopped seeing in me what I have sometimes had a hard time remembering on my own—that just being myself was the best gift I could give in return for your kindness.

Marie Palot

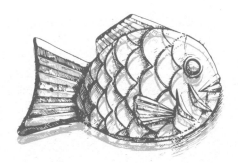

PO Box 3088
San Rafael, CA 94912
www.insighteditions.com

Find us on Facebook: www.facebook.com/InsightEditions
Follow us on X: @insighteditions
Follow us on Instagram: @insighteditions

All rights reserved. Published by Insight Editions, San Rafael, California, in 2024.

Originally published in French as *Gastronogeek - KDrama: Les Meilleures Recettes des Séries Coréennes*
by Hachette Heroes, France, in 2023. English translation by Lisa Molle Troyer. English translation © 2024
Insight Editions.

ISBN: 979-8-88663-610-9

Publisher: Raoul Goff
VP, Co-Publisher: Vanessa Lopez
VP, Creative: Chrissy Kwasnik
VP, Manufacturing: Alix Nicholaeff
VP, Group Managing Editor: Vicki Jaeger
Publishing Director: Jamie Thompson
Design Manager: Megan Sinead-Harris
Production Designer: Jean Hwang
Managing Editor: Maria Spano
Senior Production Editor: Katie Rokakis
Sponsoring Editor: Jennifer Pellman
Production Associate: Deena Hashem
Senior Production Manager, Subsidiary Rights: Lina s Palma-Temena
Illustrations: ©iStock; except pages 77 and 85: Bérengère Demoncy

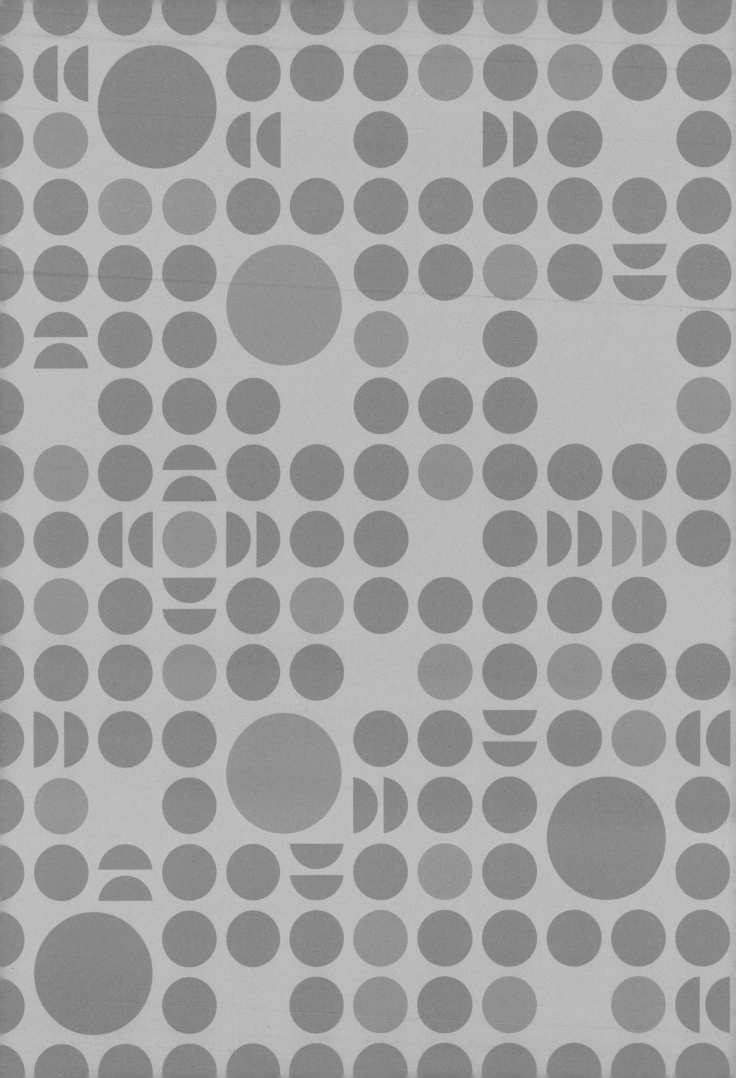